DIFFERENTIAl

LIBRARY OF MATHEMATICS

edited by

WALTER LEDERMANN

D.Sc., Ph.D., F.R.S.Ed., Professor of
Mathematics, University of Sussex

DIFFERENTIAL CALCULUS

BY

P. J. HILTON

LONDON: Routledge & Kegan Paul Ltd
NEW YORK: Dover Publications Inc.

First Published 1958
in Great Britain by
Routledge & Kegan Paul Ltd
Broadway House, 68–74 Carter Lane
London, EC4V 5EL
and in the U.S.A. by
Dover Publications Inc.
180 Varick Street
New York, 10014

Reprinted 1959, 1963, 1966, 1968 and 1974

ISBN 0 7100 4341 4

Printed in Great Britain
by Butler & Tanner Ltd
Frome and London

Preface

THIS book is intended to provide the university student in the physical sciences with information about the differential calculus which he is likely to need. The techniques described are presented with due regard for their theoretical basis; but the emphasis is on detailed discussion of the ideas of the differential calculus and on the avoidance of false statements rather than on complete proofs of all results. It is a frequent experience of the university lecturer that science students 'know how to differentiate', but are less confident when asked to say 'what $\frac{dy}{dx}$ means'. It is with the conviction that a proper understanding of the calculus is actually useful in scientific work and not merely the preoccupation of pedantic mathematicians that this book has been written.

The author wishes to thank his colleague and friend, Dr. W. Ledermann, for his invaluable suggestions during the preparation of this book.

P. J. HILTON

The University,
  Manchester

Contents

CHAPTER ONE
Introduction to Coordinate Geometry

In this introductory chapter we briefly review the basic notions which are essential to a geometrical picture of the significance of the differential calculus; thus this chapter is not concerned explicitly with the calculus and is intended for revision and reference.

Let a straight line be drawn in a given plane. Choose a fixed point, O, in the line (called the origin) and choose a direction or sense, in the line, called the positive direction. A point on the line (or axis) which precedes the origin in the positive direction is said to be on the negative side of the origin, while a point which follows the origin is said to be on the positive side. We may now represent each point on the line by a real number, or coordinate. The coordinate of a point, P, on the positive side is $+p$, where p is the length of OP, and the coordinate of a point, Q, on the negative side is $-q$, where q is the length of OQ. The origin itself, of course, has coordinate o.

Now let two mutually perpendicular lines be drawn in the plane and let their point of intersection, O, be taken as the origin on each. Choose a direction in each line, and call the lines the x-axis and y-axis (or Ox and Oy.) Then each point, P, of the plane determines—and, conversely, is determined by—an ordered pair of real numbers (a,b), where a is the coordinate of the projection of P on the x-axis and b is the coordinate of the projection of P on the y-axis. We call a the x-coordinate, b the y-coordinate, and (a,b) the coordinates of P. If, as usual, we take the x-axis horizontal directed from left to right, and the y-axis vertical directed from bottom to top, then the relation between points and coordinates is demonstrated in Fig. 1. The system we have described is called the Cartesian coordinate system of the plane; the name 'Cartesian' refers to Rene Descartes (1596–1650), the French mathematician who played a leading part in the invention and development of coordinate geometry. It is customary and convenient[1] simply

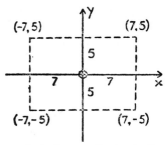

FIG. I.—Cartesian coordinates in the plane.

to refer to 'the point (a,b)' instead of 'the point whose co-ordinates are (a,b)'; this practice is satisfactory so long as we do not change the coordinate system, and we will adopt it. Thus we may say briefly that the distance between (a_1,b_1) and (a_2,b_2) may be shown by Pythagoras' theorem to be

$$\sqrt{(a_2-a_1)^2+(b_2-b_1)^2}. \qquad (\text{I.I})$$

Curves in the plane are sets of points, or sets of pairs (x,y). Thus to every curve corresponds some equation connecting x and y, and conversely to every equation corresponds the set of points whose coordinates satisfy it. In this correspondence, linear equations

$$ax+by+c=0, \qquad (\text{I.2})$$

where not both of a,b are zero, correspond to straight lines in the plane. If $b=0$, the equation is $x=-\dfrac{c}{a}$, representing a line parallel to the y-axis. If $b\neq0$, we may divide by b, getting, say,

$$y=mx+d.$$

This is a line with gradient m cutting off an intercept d on

[1] Practices can be customary but inconvenient; we include in this category the description of the x-coordinate as 'abscissa' and the y-coordinate as 'ordinate'.

the y-axis; notice that, for convenience, we 'identify' a line with its equation. The straight line joining (x_1, y_1) to (x_2, y_2) is given by the equation

$$\frac{x-x_1}{x_2-x_1} = \frac{y-y_1}{y_2-y_1}, \tag{1.3}$$

and its gradient is

$$\frac{y_2-y_1}{x_2-x_2}. \tag{1.4}$$

The point of intersection of two non-parallel lines is simply obtained by solving the corresponding equations. We know that the solution must be unique[1] and we have now obtained a geometrical interpretation of this fact, together with a geometrical interpretation of the exceptional case (thus the equations $a_1x+b_1y+c_1=0$, $a_2x+b_2y+c_2=0$ do not have a unique solution if $\frac{a_1}{a_2}=\frac{b_1}{b_2}$, which means that the lines either coincide or are parallel). More generally, we may identify solutions of a pair of simultaneous equations in x and y with the points of intersection of the corresponding curves.

Other coordinate systems may be used to describe the position of a point in the plane. Of particular importance are polar coordinates. Choose an axis and a point, O, on it; choose a positive direction on the axis. Then any point P in the plane may be described by its distance from O (say, r) and the angle which OP makes with the positive direction of the axis (say, θ). In elementary trigonometry it is customary to measure angles between 0° and 360°; however, it will suit us better to reduce angles between 180° and 360° by 360°, so that the angle θ will be taken to lie between $-180°$ (excluded) and $+180°$ (included). Then every point in the plane except the origin determines a unique pair of polar coordinates (r, θ); the origin, however, may be represented by $(0, \theta)$, for any θ.

If we identify the given axis with the positive direction of

---

[1] See, e.g., P. M. Cohn, *Linear Equations*, in this series.

the x-axis, and the point O with the origin, the two coordinate systems are related by

$$x = r \cos \theta, \; y = r \sin \theta; \tag{1.5}$$

inversely, r is uniquely determined as the positive (or zero) square root of $x^2 + y^2$, and, away from the origin, θ is uniquely determined by $\cos \theta = \dfrac{x}{r}$, $\sin \theta = \dfrac{y}{r}$.

The equations of some curves are more conveniently expressed in polar coordinates than in Cartesian coordinates. This is notably true for circles, centre O. If the radius of the circle is a, then the (x,y) equation is $x^2 + y^2 = a^2$, while the (r,θ) equation is $r = a$.

PARAMETERS

We have seen that a curve in the (x,y)-plane is given by an equation connecting x and y. On the other hand, we may express the coordinates of a general point on a curve by means of a pair of functions $(f(t), g(t))$ of a *single* variable t; thus, for example, the general point on the circle, centre O, radius a, is $(a \cos t, a \sin t)$. In this example, the *parameter* t represents the 'θ' coordinate of the point (see Fig. 2). In general, the equation

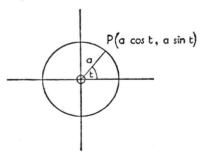

FIG. 2.—The circle $x^2 + y^2 = a^2$ parametrized by angular coordinate t.

of the curve may be obtained by eliminating t between the equations $x = f(t)$, $y = g(t)$. The variable t may be thought of as a coordinate *on the curve*, since to any value of t there corresponds a point on the curve and, conversely, the coordinates of any point on the curve are expressible as $(f(t), g(t))$ for some value of t. Thus the parameter t is also called a current co-ordinate on the curve.[1] To express a curve by means of a para-meter or current coordinate is to *parametrize* the curve. Thus we may parametrize the parabola $y^2 = 4ax$ by $(at^2, 2at)$. It is frequently more convenient to work with a parameter, since then the fact that a point lies on the curve is already contained in the expressions for its coordinates. A second advantage of the parametric form lies in the fact that the coordinates x and y of a point then play symmetric roles in so far as each is a vari-able dependent on the independent variable t, whereas in the form $y = f(x)$ the y-coordinate is made dependent on the x-coordinate. This feature of the parametric form is exemplified by the circle discussed above; of course, it is possible to avoid the form $y = f(x)$ in this case by adopting the form $x^2 + y^2 = a^2$, but this, too, has defects compared with the parametric form. A third practical advantage of the parametric form lies in the fact that it may be extremely inconvenient to eliminate the parameter. Thus the equation of the cycloid is given para-metrically by $x = a(t + \sin t)$, $y = a(1 + \cos t)$. It is unnecessary surely to stress how unpleasant the equation would be if t were eliminated!

To stress the fact that the Cartesian coordinates (x, y) are functions of a parameter t it is common practice to write $(x(t), y(t))$ for the coordinates in the general case.

[1] For example, in differential geometry, we frequently take arc length, measured from a fixed point on the curve, as current coordinate.

5

CHAPTER TWO

Rate of Change and Differentiation

I. THE MEANING OF 'RATE OF CHANGE'

THE differential calculus was invented by Isaac Newton in the years 1664-5 to give a precise mathematical formulation to the laws of motion. Let us recall Newton's three laws of motion: they are

(1) Every body will continue in its state of rest or uniform motion in a straight line unless acted on by an impressed force;

(2) Rate of change of momentum is proportional to the impressed force and takes place in the line of action of the impressed force;

(3) Action and reaction are equal and opposite.

The essential idea underlying these statements is that of 'rate of change', and it is this idea which gave rise to the basic notion of the differential calculus. Let us consider the following simple example. Suppose a train covers a distance of 180 miles in 3 hours. Then the average speed is 60 m.p.h. This is obvious in two senses; first the calculation is trivially easy, and second the meaning to be attached to the statement is clear. However, suppose we wish to say what the speed of the train was as it passed a point P on its route; it is then by no means clear what this 'speed' signifies. If the train had been in a state of 'uniform motion' throughout its journey, the speed on passing P would, of course, have been 60 m.p.h., but it is certain that forces did act on the train and consequently the motion would not have been uniform. A man may stand with a stopwatch and observe that the train travels from P to a point Q, 220 yards further down the track, in 10 seconds, and so assert that its speed on passing P was 45 m.p.h.; but clearly this is still only an average speed, even though for practical purposes no more accurate measure of the speed at P may be desirable or even possible. Thus whatever meaning (if any) is to be given to the phrase 'speed at P' it is at least clear that we must insist that we get nearer to it the shorter the time (or the distance) over which we reckon the average speed.

In practice, we can often do no better than calculate a reasonable average speed; but we should be able to improve our estimate further by plotting distance travelled against time taken on a graph. Assuming we have taken sufficient 'readings', we may join up the points corresponding to the readings by a smooth curve[1] and so get a picture of the distance–time relationship. Two points Q_1, Q_2 on the curve with coordinates (a_1, b_1), (a_2, b_2), correspond to points P_1, P_2 on the route, respectively b_1, b_2 miles from the starting point and reached after a_1, a_2 hours of travelling. The average speed over the stretch $P_1 P_2$ is

$$\frac{b_2 - b_1}{a_2 - a_1} \text{ m.p.h.,}$$

and we would accept this as a reasonable estimate of the speed at P_1 if P_2 is taken near to P_1, the nearer the better. Now $\frac{b_2 - b_1}{a_2 - a_1}$ is precisely the gradient of the chord $Q_1 Q_2$ (see Fig. 3). As P_2 approaches P_1 (that is, as we take P_2 closer and closer to P_1), Q_2 approaches Q_1, and we have an intuitive picture of the chord $Q_1 Q_2$ moving round into a limiting position, that occupied by the tangent to the curve at Q_1. It would thus appear reasonable to define the speed at P_1 as the gradient of the tangent to the space–time curve at the corresponding point Q_1. It is indeed highly significant that the German mathematician Leibniz, who invented the differential calculus almost simultaneously with, but independently of, Newton, did not have in mind primarily the question of speed and rates of change, but was concerned particularly with the problem of obtaining a formula for the gradient of the tangent to a curve at an arbitrary point

[1] We are assuming that the train is an express and not a slow train stopping at stations!

7

on it. We see that, in effect, the two approaches are equivalent. However, Leibniz assumed (in order to give his problem meaning) that the curve under investigation was itself given by a

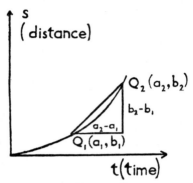

FIG. 3.—Distance–time curve.

formula. Thus we may suppose that the relationship between distance travelled, s, and time taken, t, is expressed by a law of the form

$$s = f(t) \qquad (2.1)$$

where f is some mathematical function. Having decided the *conceptual* question of what is meant by the 'speed at time t (or distance s)', there remains the *mathematical* problem of how to calculate the speed from the relationship (2.1) without having to resort to the procedure of drawing a graph; in any case, the latter can only produce an approximate answer. It was Newton's supreme triumph that he not only gave the formulae expressing the laws of motion and the law of universal gravitation, but also created the mathematical machinery, namely the differential and integral calculus, by which precise deductions could be made from these laws.

Let us take a second example. Suppose it is discovered experimentally that a body falling in vacuo falls a distance of $16t^2$ feet in t seconds. The relationship (2.1) then becomes

$$= s16t^2.$$

If the graph is plotted and the curve $s = 16t^2$ drawn (we would have a t-axis instead of an x-axis and an s-axis instead of a y-axis) it is easy to see that the gradient of the chord joining (t_1, s_1) to (t_2, s_2) is

$$\frac{16(t_2^2 - t_1^2)}{t_2 - t_1} = 16(t_2 + t_1).$$

Moreover, this formula holds even if t_2 is less than t_1. Thus the speed at time t_1 is 'approximately' $16(t_2 + t_1)$ feet per second, where t_2 is near to t_1. Now obviously the closer we take t_2 to t_1, the nearer does $16(t_2 + t_1)$ get to $32t_1$. Thus we are led to believe that the gradient of the tangent to the curve at (t_1, s_1) is $32t_1$ and, equivalently, that the speed of the body after travelling for t_1 seconds is $32t_1$ feet per second. For the time being there is nothing here which we can *prove*; for on the one hand we have not defined precisely the notion of the 'limiting position of a chord' and on the other hand we have not defined precisely the notion of the 'speed at time t'. In the next section we provide the necessary definitions in accordance with our intuitive picture, in such a way that the equivalence between the notion of gradient of a tangent and the notion of speed is preserved. More generally, when one variable y depends on a second variable x, so that we may write

$$y = f(x),$$

we will define a quantity, $f'(a)$, which will measure the rate of change of y with x at the point a (i.e. at the point on the curve whose x-coordinate is a). The process of obtaining this quantity is called differentiation and thus differentiation gives us, in particular, the necessary technique for calculating the speed of a moving body when we know the distance–time relationship.

2. LIMITS

Let us briefly review the second example discussed above. We observed that the average speed of the falling body in the interval of time between t_1 and t_2 was $16(t_1 + t_2)$ feet per second. Let us write $t_2 = t_1 + h$ (where h will be negative if t_2 is less than t_1). Then the average speed is $(32t_1 + 16h)$ feet per second. We now remark that the quantity $32t_1 + 16h$ may be brought as near as we please to $32t_1$ by taking h sufficiently small. For example, it is within $\cdot 1$ of $32t_1$ if h is in absolute value[1] less than $\cdot 00625$, and it is within $\cdot 001$ of $32t_1$ if h is in absolute value less than $\cdot 0000625$. Thus the average speed may be brought as near to $32t_1$ as we please. There is therefore no doubt that we should say that the speed at time t_1 is $32t_1$ feet per second and that no other value is conceivable. We stress here that what we have been saying is very different from the statement that the value of $32t_1 + 16h$ for $h=0$ is $32t_1$; we have been concerned with the values of this function in the 'neighbourhood' of $h=0$, i.e., for small, but non-zero, values of h. In fact, using the mathematical concept of a limit, defined below, we will pick out the value of $32t_1$ for the speed, and the definition will be such that the value of $32t_1 + 16h$ at $h=0$ will not come into the question at all!

Since the idea of a limit is not to be thought of as applying exclusively to the concept of quantities varying with time, we will, as usual, use the symbols x for the independent variable, y for the dependent variable. Then

$$y = f(x)$$

represents the fact that the value of y is given in terms of the value of x by means of the function f. We will always assume that a function is defined for all real values of x (unless otherwise stated) and takes real values.

Definition 2.1. *We say that $f(x)$ tends to the limit l as x tends to a if the difference between $f(x)$ and l remains as small as we please so long as x remains sufficiently near to a, while remaining distinct from a.*

We write $f(x) \rightarrow l$ as $x \rightarrow a$ or $\lim_{x \to a} f(x) = l$. Notice again that this is not the same thing as saying that $f(a) = l$; in fact, the value of $f(a)$ is quite irrelevant to the question of the value of l and it is not even necessary for $f(x)$ to have been defined at $x = a$; for example, we will show later that $\lim_{x \to 0} \dfrac{\sin x}{x} = 1$ but $\dfrac{\sin x}{x}$ is not defined at $x=0$. On the other hand, in most cases

[1]i.e., if h lies between $\pm \cdot 00625$.

that the student is likely to meet when one variable is given as a function of another, the limit l exists and equals $f(a)$. Such functions are of tremendous importance in mathematics and we have the

Definition 2.2. *We say that $f(x)$ is continuous at $x=a$ if $\lim_{x \to a} f(x)$ exists and equals $f(a)$.*

We remark that, had we not included the phrase 'while remaining distinct from a' in Definition 2.1, the notion of limit would have been immensely restricted since only functions defined and continuous at $x=a$ could tend to a limit as x tended to a. Such a restriction would, indeed, have had disastrous consequences for our main aim of defining differentiation.

We now give two examples to illustrate how 'things can go wrong'. Our first example is of the non-existence of a limit. Let x be time and let y be the age of Mr. A on his last birthday. Let a be the date of Mr. A's 30th birthday. Then y is a function of x, $y=f(x)$, and $f(x)=29$ if x is near to but less than a, while $f(x)=30$ if x is near to but greater than a. Thus there is no candidate for $\lim_{x \to a} f(x)$, since $f(x)$ takes the values 29 and 30 arbitrarily close to a. This is actually a case in which $f(x)$ has a limit from the left (29) and a limit from the right (30) which are, of course, different; it is easy to see that $\lim_{x \to a} f(x)$ exists and equals l if and only if the limits from left and right both exist and are equal to l.

Our second example is of a function $f(x)$ such that $\lim_{x \to a} f(x)$ exists but is different from $f(a)$. Suppose an electrical pulse of unit strength is transmitted along a short wire each second. Then if we plot current, y, against time, x, measured in seconds, we get (approximately) a function $y=f(x)$ where

$$y=1 \text{ if } x=0,1,2, \ldots ,$$
$$y=0, \text{ otherwise.}$$

Then $\lim_{x \to 1} f(x)=0$, but $f(1)=1$. Having given these two examples by way of warning, we will henceforth assume, unless otherwise stated, that limits under discussion exist and that functions under discussion are continuous.

We now achieve our main objective, namely

Definition 2.3. *The differential coefficient at $x=a$ of the function $f(x)$ is*

$$\lim_{x \to a} \frac{f(x)-f(a)}{x-a}.$$

We remark that it is a matter of indifference to us in this definition that the function $\dfrac{f(x)-f(a)}{x-a}$ is undefined at $x=a$; we are only concerned with the behaviour of the function near a. We write $f'(a)$ for the differential coefficient of $f(x)$ at $x=a$ and $f'(x)$ for the function whose value at $x=a$ is $f'(a)$. The process of passing from $f(x)$ to $f'(x)$ is known as differentiation and $f'(x)$ is called the derivative of $f(x)$. Before proceeding to give examples, we make the important observation that, writing $x-a=h$, we have

$$\lim_{h \to 0} \frac{f(a+h)-f(a)}{h}=f'(a) \tag{2.2}$$

This formulation is, in fact, the one which will appear most frequently in the sequel. Notice that it is an immediate consequence of (2.2) that the derivative of a constant is zero.

Example 2.1. Let $f(x)=x$. Then $\dfrac{f(a+h)-f(a)}{h}=\dfrac{(a+h)-a}{h}=1$,

so that

$$\lim_{h \to 0} \frac{f(a+h)-f(a)}{h}=1.$$

Thus $f'(x)=1$.

Example 2.2. Let $f(x)=16x^2$. Then

$$\frac{f(a+h)-f(a)}{h}=\frac{16(a+h)^2-16a^2}{h}=32a+16h.$$

Then $\lim\limits_{h \to 0} \dfrac{f(a+h)-f(a)}{h}=32a$, so that $f'(a)=32a$, whence

$$f'(x)=32x.$$

12

This second example sets the seal on our attempt to attribute speed to a falling body. It shows that the speed, *v*, of the body is related to time by the formula

$$v = 32t,$$

as already suggested. In order to obtain agreement with the definition of speed by means of the gradient of the tangent to a curve, we adopt the definition

Definition 2.4. *The tangent to the curve* $y = f(x)$ *at the point* (a,b) *on the curve is the line through* (a,b) *with gradient* $f'(a)$.

Then the tangent is certainly the limiting position of chords through (a,b) in the precise sense that its gradient is the limit of the gradients of such chords. We will see in the next chapter that the tangent does have the property usually associated with it.

The main difficulty of the calculus is now over. In subsequent sections and chapters we will be concerned purely with technical questions, rules for differentiating, and uses of the calculus. We have taken some time to describe carefully the conceptual aspect of the calculus since it has so often been misunderstood. In particular it is often thought that the calculus is a means of giving significance to the meaningless expression $\dfrac{0}{0}$ $\Big($obtained,

e.g., by 'substituting' *a* for *x* in $\dfrac{f(x)-f(a)}{x-a}$!$\Big)$. This impression has been fostered by the use of a notation (see (2.5) below) which, though valuable, does lend itself to confusion. We close this section by discussing this and other notational questions.

We revert to the curve $y = f(x)$ and consider two points (a,b), $(a+h, b+k)$ on it. Then $b = f(a)$, $b+k = f(a+h)$, so that $k = f(a+h) - f(a)$ and

$$\frac{k}{h} = \frac{f(a+h) - f(a)}{h} \tag{2.3}$$

By (2.2) and (2.3), we see that

$$f'(a) = \lim_{h \to 0} \frac{k}{h}.$$

Now we may see easily that such a limit exists only if k is small when h is small, that is, only if k tends to o as h tends to o; but this is precisely equivalent to the condition that $f(x)$ is continuous at $x=a$. Thus we may think of h as a small (positive or negative) increment in x and k as the corresponding small increment in y. If, as is customary, we write $\delta x, \delta y$ for h, k we have $y=f(x)$, $y+\delta y=f(x+\delta x)$, and

$$f'(x)=\lim_{\delta x \to 0} \frac{\delta y}{\delta x};\tag{2.4}$$

here, the role of x is left somewhat obscure in some text-books —we emphasize that it must be regarded as signifying a *fixed* but arbitrary value of the independent variable (corresponding to a in our notation) and not as the variable itself. However, the next stage, *which is purely notational*, has often proved the most baffling. It is customary to write $\frac{dy}{dx}$ for $\lim_{\delta x \to 0} \frac{\delta y}{\delta x}$, so that

$$\frac{dy}{dx}=f'(x)\tag{2.5}$$

Indeed, some authors refer to dx as the 'limit of the infinitesimal increment δx' and dy as the 'limit of the infinitesimal increment δy'; unfortunately, this nonsense appears to mean something, namely that $dx=0$ and $dy=0$, so that $\frac{dy}{dx}=\frac{0}{0}$!! Notice that we make no use whatsoever of the term 'infinitesimal' and have no difficulty in avoiding the pitfalls of this lunatic logic. For us, $\frac{dy}{dx}$ is simply another notation for the derivative of y with respect to x when y is given as a function of x; we refer to this as the Leibniz notation. We may think of $\frac{d}{dx}$ as the operation transforming a function into its derivative.

Since $f'(x)$ is itself a function of x, we may consider its derivative; this is written $f''(x)$. So we may continue (assuming, of course, our functions remain differentiable); the nth derivative is usually written $f^{(n)}(x)$. In the Leibniz notation, we write

$\dfrac{d^2y}{dx^2}, \dfrac{d^3y}{dx^3}, \ldots, \dfrac{d^ny}{dx^n}$. The derivatives $f^{(n)}(x)$ with $n \geqslant 2$ are called the higher derivatives.

Example 2.2. Reverting to this example, we see that if $f(x)=16x^2$, then $f''(x)=32$. Now interpreting x as time and $y=f(x)$ as distance, then $f''(x)$ is rate of change of velocity ($f'(x)$) with time, or acceleration. Thus the acceleration of the body is 32 feet per second per second.

Finally, we mention two other notations. In the first, we write D for $\dfrac{d}{dx}$, so that $Dy=\dfrac{dy}{dx}$, $Df=f'$. This operational notation (so-called because D operates on a function to produce its derivative) should only be used when there is no doubt as to which symbol stands for the independent variable. The higher derivatives are written

$$D^2y, \ldots D^ny; \text{ thus } D^ny=D(D(D(\ldots (Dy)\ldots).$$

The second notation, which the reader will probably meet in text-books on dynamics, is reserved for differentiation with respect to time. Then $\dfrac{dx}{dt}$ is written $\dot{x}$, $\dfrac{d^2x}{dt^2}$ is written $\ddot{x}$; this notation is due to Newton.

3. RULES FOR DIFFERENTIATING

In this section we establish the basic facts about the differentiation process. We tacitly assume that all functions under discussion are differentiable.

The basic facts in question are consequences of the following theorem on composite limits, which we do not prove here.[1] Its conclusions are eminently reasonable.

Theorem 2.1. *Let* $F(x) \to l$, $G(x) \to m$ *as* $x \to a$. *Then*

(i) *if* $S(x)=A.F(x)+B.G(x)$, *where* A,B *are constants*, $S(x) \to Al+Bm$ *as* $x \to a$;

(ii) *if* $P(x)=F(x)G(x)$, *then* $P(x) \to lm$ *as* $x \to a$;

(iii) *if* $Q(x)=1/G(x)$ *and* $m \neq 0$, *then* $Q(x) \to 1/m$ *as* $x \to a$.

[1] Compare corresponding theorems for the limits of sequences; see J. A. Green, *Sequences and Series*, in this series.

We apply this theorem to prove the following three theorems.

Theorem 2.2. *If* $s(x) = A.f(x) + B.g(x)$, *then*
$$s'(x) = A.f'(x) + B.g'(x).$$

For
$$\frac{s(a+h) - s(a)}{h} = \frac{Af(a+h) + Bg(a+h) - Af(a) - Bg(a)}{h}$$

$$= A.\frac{f(a+h) - f(a)}{h} + B.\frac{g(a+h) - g(a)}{h}.$$

Thus, by Theorem 2.1 (i).

$$s'(a) = \lim_{h \to 0} \frac{s(a+h) - s(a)}{h}$$

$$= A.\lim_{h \to 0} \frac{f(a+h) - f(a)}{h} + B.\lim_{h \to 0} \frac{g(a+h) - g(a)}{h} = Af'(a) + Bg'(a).$$

Since this holds for all a, the theorem follows.

Theorem 2.3. *If* $p(x) = f(x)g(x)$, *then* $p'(x) = f(x)g'(x) + f'(x)g(x)$.

For

$$\frac{p(a+h) - p(a)}{h} = \frac{f(a+h)g(a+h) - f(a)g(a)}{h}$$

$$= \frac{f(a+h)(g(a+h) - g(a))}{h} + \frac{(f(a+h) - f(a))g(a)}{h}.$$

Now $f(a+h) \to f(a)$ as $h \to 0$, since $f(x)$ is continuous at $x = a$, and $\frac{g(a+h) - g(a)}{h} \to g'(a)$ as $h \to 0$. Thus, by Theorem 2.1 (ii),

$$\frac{f(a+h)(g(a+h) - g(a))}{h} \to f(a)g'(a).$$

Since $\frac{f(a+h) - f(a)}{h} \to f'(a)$, Theorem 2.1 (i) yields

$$p'(a) = f(a)g'(a) + f'(a)g(a),$$

and the theorem follows.

Theorem 2.4. *If* $q(x) = f(x)/g(x)$, *then*
$$q'(x) = \{g(x)f'(x) - f(x)g'(x)\} / \{g(x)\}^2.$$

Before we prove this, we remark that $q(x)$ is only defined

where $g(x)$ is distinct from 0. Now we may prove this by a trick. For $f(x) = q(x)g(x)$, so that

$$f'(x) = q(x)g'(x) + q'(x)g(x).$$

Multiplying by $g(x)$, we have $g(x)f'(x) = f(x)g'(x) + q'(x)(g(x))^2$, whence the theorem follows. The reader is recommended to prove this theorem direct from Theorem 2.1.

Theorems 2.2 and 2.3 have important generalizations to higher derivatives. Clearly, the generalization of Theorem 2.2 is

Theorem 2.2(n) $D^n(A.f + B.g) = A.D^nf + B.D^ng.$

We will prove, still using this convenient notation,

Theorem 2.3(n) $D^n(fg) = D^nf.g + \binom{n}{1}D^{n-1}f.Dg + \ldots$

$$+ \binom{n}{r}D^{n-r}f.D^rg + \ldots + f.D^ng.$$

Here the expressions $\binom{n}{r}$ are binomial coefficients; in fact, the reader will notice how reminiscent the formula for $D^n(fg)$ is of the binomial expansion. The formula was discovered by Leibniz and is known as Leibniz' formula. The proof is very similar to that of the binomial theorem and proceeds by induction on n. For $n = 1$, we have just Theorem 2.3; so we suppose the formula holds for $n = k$. Then

$$D^{k+1}(fg) = D(D^k(fg)) = D\{D^kf.g + \ldots + \binom{k}{r-1}D^{k-r+1}f.D^{r-1}g$$

$$+ \binom{k}{r}D^{k-r}f.D^rg + \ldots + f.D^kg\}$$

$$= D^{k+1}f.g + \ldots + \left(\binom{k}{r-1} + \binom{k}{r}\right)D^{k+1-r}f.D^rg + \ldots + f.D^{k+1}g,$$

by Theorem 2.3,

$$= D^{k+1}f.g + \ldots + \binom{k+1}{r}D^{k+1-r}f.D^rg + \ldots + f.D^{k+1}g,$$

17

in view of the easily proved relation

$$\binom{k}{r-1}+\binom{k}{r}=\binom{k+1}{r}.$$

Thus the formula also holds for $n=k+1$, and so for all values of n.

Example 2.3. $D^n(xg)=xD^ng+nD^{n-1}g$.

For we know that $Dx=1$, and, as already remarked, the derivative ('rate of change') of any constant is zero. Thus $D^mx=0$, $m>1$. Then the only terms in the Leibniz formula (with f replaced by x) which are different from zero are the last two.

Our next rule for differentiating is of a different nature. Suppose that y is a differentiable function of z and z is a differentiable function of x. Then y is a function of x; indeed, it is a differentiable function of x. The best way of proving this is to give the explicit formula for $\dfrac{dy}{dx}$, namely

Theorem 2.5. $\dfrac{dy}{dx}=\dfrac{dy}{dz}\dfrac{dz}{dx}$.

Let $y=f(z)$ and $z=g(x)$; we wish to prove that

$$\lim_{h\to 0}\frac{f(g(a+h))-f(g(a))}{h}=f'(g(a)).g'(a).$$

Now, by definition, $\lim_{h\to 0}\dfrac{g(a+h)-g(a)}{h}=g'(a)$; this is precisely equivalent to the statement

$$g(a+h)=g(a)+h(g'(a)+\varepsilon(h)) \tag{2.6}$$

where $\varepsilon(h)$ is a function of h which tends to o as $h\to 0$.

Put $g(a)=b$, $g(a+h)=b+k$. Then $k\to 0$ as $h\to 0$. Moreover, $f(b+k)=f(b)+k(f'(b)+\eta(k))$, where $\eta(k)\to 0$ as $k\to 0$. Thus
$$\begin{aligned}
f(b+k)-f(b)&=k(f'(b)+\eta(k))=(g(a+h)-g(a))(f'(b)+\eta(k))\\
&=h(g'(a)+\varepsilon(h))(f'(b)+\eta(k))\\
&=h(g'(a)f'(b)+\mu(h)),
\end{aligned}$$
where $\mu(h)=\varepsilon(h)f'(b)+g'(a)\eta(k)+\varepsilon(h)\eta(k)$ and thus tends to o

as $h \to 0$. We have proved that $\dfrac{f(b+k)-f(b)}{h} \to g'(a)f'(b)$ as $h \to 0$, and this is precisely what was to be proved.

The Leibniz notation makes this theorem look far more obvious than it really is. A proof may be given by invoking the truly trivial statement $\dfrac{\delta y}{\delta x} = \dfrac{\delta y}{\delta z}\,\dfrac{\delta z}{\delta x}$ and taking limits but there are difficulties associated with possible zero values of δz.

There is no convenient generalization of Theorem 2.5 to higher derivatives. As an example we will show that $\dfrac{d^2y}{dx^2}$ is not equal to $\dfrac{d^2y}{dz^2}\,\dfrac{d^2z}{dx^2}$.

Example 2.4. $\dfrac{d^2y}{dx^2} = \dfrac{d^2y}{dz^2}\left(\dfrac{dz}{dx}\right)^2 + \dfrac{dy}{dz}\,\dfrac{d^2z}{dx^2}$.

For $\dfrac{d^2y}{dx^2} = \dfrac{d}{dx}\left(\dfrac{dy}{dx}\right) = \dfrac{d}{dx}\left(\dfrac{dy}{dz} \cdot \dfrac{dz}{dx}\right)$

$$= \dfrac{d}{dx}\left(\dfrac{dy}{dz}\right) \cdot \dfrac{dz}{dx} + \dfrac{dy}{dz} \cdot \dfrac{d^2z}{dx^2},\ \text{by Theorem 2.3.}$$

Again, by Theorem 2.5, $\dfrac{d}{dx}\left(\dfrac{dy}{dz}\right) = \dfrac{d}{dz}\left(\dfrac{dy}{dz}\right)\dfrac{dz}{dx}$ $\left(\text{we replace } y \text{ in}\right.$ Theorem 2.5 by $\left.\dfrac{dy}{dz}\right)$. Thus $\dfrac{d}{dx}\left(\dfrac{dy}{dz}\right) = \dfrac{d^2y}{dz^2}\,\dfrac{dz}{dx}$, and the formula is demonstrated.

A most important special case of Theorem 2.5 is the following. Suppose, for a given range of values of x, the function $f(x)$ is one–one. That is to say, suppose that, in this range, different values of x give rise to different values of $f(x)$. Then x may be considered as a function of y over this range. Suppose, to be precise, that $f(x)$ is a one–one function from the interval $x_0 \leqslant x \leqslant x_1$ on to the interval $y_0 \leqslant y \leqslant y_1$. Then we may define a (one–one) function from the interval $y_0 \leqslant y \leqslant y_1$ on to the interval $x_0 \leqslant x \leqslant x_1$ by associating, with any such y, the value of x such that $f(x) = y$. This new function from y to x is called the inverse of the function f (see Fig. 4). For example, if $y = ax + b$, then $x = \dfrac{y-b}{a}$; here we may take for our intervals the entire x- and y-axes. On the other hand, $y=x^2$ is a one–one function of the semi-infinite interval $x \geqslant 0$ on the semi-infinite interval $y \geqslant 0$; as such, it has an inverse, namely $x = +\sqrt{y}$. It is not, of course, one–one on the whole x-axis, since $(-x)^2 = x^2$. Let

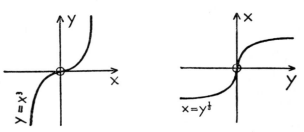

FIG. 4.—Function $(y = x^3)$ and its inverse $(x = y^{\frac{1}{3}})$.

us write $x = g(y)$ for the function inverse to $y = f(x)$. Then we may apply Theorem 2.5 in the form $\dfrac{dy}{dy} = \dfrac{dy}{dx} \cdot \dfrac{dx}{dy}$; but $\dfrac{dy}{dy} = 1$, so that

$$\frac{dx}{dy} = 1 \bigg/ \frac{dy}{dx}; \tag{2.7}$$

otherwise expressed, if a is any interior[1] point of the interval $x_0 \leqslant x \leqslant x_1$, and $b = f(a)$, then b is an interior point of $y_0 \leqslant y \leqslant y_1$, and

$$g'(b) = 1/f'(a). \tag{2.8}$$

Notice, from (2.7), that it is possible that $\dfrac{dx}{dy}$ may not exist, because $\dfrac{dy}{dx} = 0$ at some point $x = a$. For example, $y = x^3$ is one–one on the whole x-axis with inverse $x = y^{\frac{1}{3}}$; but since $\dfrac{dy}{dx} = 0$ at $x = 0$, $\dfrac{dx}{dy}$ does not exist at $y = 0$. On the other hand it may

[1] i.e., distinct from x_0 or x_1.

20

readily be shown that if $f'(x)$ is continuous and $f'(a) \neq 0$, then $y = f(x)$ is one-one near $x = a$ and that the inverse is differentiable, the differential coefficient at $y = b = f(a)$ being given by (2.8). The reader is advised to satisfy himself that (2.7) is really an immediate application of Theorem 2.1 (iii).

Example 2.5. If $y = +\sqrt{x}$, then $\dfrac{dy}{dx} = \dfrac{1}{2\sqrt{x}}$, for any positive x.

For $x = y^2, \dfrac{dx}{dy} = 2y$ (see Example 2.2, or verify directly),

$$\frac{dy}{dx} = \frac{1}{2y} = \frac{1}{2\sqrt{x}}.$$

Theorem 2.5 often appears in the following form: given y as a function of x, so that $\dfrac{dy}{dx}$ is known, to find $\dfrac{d}{dx} f(y)$. The conclusion is

$$\frac{d}{dx} f(y) = f'(y) \frac{dy}{dx} \qquad (2 \cdot 9)$$

4. FORMULAE FOR DIFFERENTIATING

In this section we obtain formulae for the differential coefficients of standard functions.

(i) *Polynomials and fractional powers*

A polynomial is a function of the form

$$a_0 x^n + a_1 x^{n-1} + \ldots + a_n.$$

By Theorem 2.2, to differentiate this it is sufficient to know the derivative of x^n, for arbitrary positive integers n. In fact, we obtain a more general result, namely

Formula 2.1. $\dfrac{d}{dx} x^n = n x^{n-1}$, *where n is any rational number.*

Recall that a rational number is the ratio of two integers. However, we will first prove the formula if n is an integer.

It is certainly true if $n = 0, 1$; we prove it for positive integers

n by induction. Suppose, then, that $\frac{d}{dx}x^k = kx^{k-1}$. Then by Theorem 2.3,

$$\frac{d}{dx}(x^{k+1}) = \frac{d}{dx}(x^k . x) = kx^{k-1} . x + x^k . 1 = (k+1)x^k.$$

Thus the formula holds for $n = k+1$, and so, by induction, for all positive integers n.

Now let $n = -m$, where m is a positive integer. Then, if $y = x^n$, $yx^m = 1$. Differentiating, we have $\frac{dy}{dx} . x^m + y . mx^{m-1} = 0$, by Theorem 2.3, or $x\frac{dy}{dx} + my = 0$. Replacing m by $-n$ and y by x^n, we have $x\frac{dy}{dx} - nx^n = 0$, whence

$$\frac{dy}{dx} = nx^{n-1}.$$

Finally let $n = \frac{p}{q}$, where p, q are integers. Then, if $y = x^n$, $y^q = x^p$. Differentiating and using (2.9), we have

$$qy^{q-1}\frac{dy}{dx} = px^{p-1}.$$

Thus $\frac{dy}{dx} = n . \frac{x^{p-1}}{y^{q-1}} = n . \frac{x^{p-1}y}{x^p} = n . \frac{y}{x} = nx^{n-1}$, and the formula has been proved in general.

Example 2.6. Differentiate $\frac{x + x^{\frac{1}{2}}}{1 + 4x^2}$.

Applying Theorem 2.4, we have that the derivative is

$$\frac{(1+4x^2)\left(1 + \frac{1}{2x^{\frac{1}{2}}}\right) - (x + x^{\frac{1}{2}}) . 8x}{(1+4x^2)^2} = \frac{1 + 2x^{\frac{1}{2}} - 12x^2 - 8x^{\frac{5}{2}}}{2x^{\frac{1}{2}}(1+4x^2)^2}.$$

Example 2.7. $\frac{d^m}{dx^m}(ax+b)^n = a^m \frac{n!}{(n-m)!}(ax+b)^{n-m}$, where $n \geqslant m \geqslant 0$.

We may prove this by induction on m; notice that it is perfectly legitimate to start the induction at $m=0$, interpreting $\frac{d^0}{dx^0}f(x)$ simply as $f(x)$. Suppose then that the formula holds for $m=k<n$. Then

$$\frac{d^{k+1}}{dx^{k+1}}(ax+b)^n=a^k\frac{n!}{(n-k)!}\frac{d}{dx}(ax+b)^{n-k}.$$

Now put $z=ax+b$; then $\frac{dz}{dx}=a$, and, if $y=z^{n-k}$,

$$\frac{dy}{dz}=(n-k)z^{n-k-1}.$$

Thus if $y=(ax+b)^{n-k}$, $\frac{dy}{dx}=\frac{dy}{dz}\cdot\frac{dz}{dx}=a(n-k)(ax+b)^{n-k-1}$. We have therefore shown that

$$\frac{d^{k+1}}{dx^{k+1}}(ax+b)^n=a^{k+1}\frac{n!}{(n-k-1)!}(ax+b)^{n-k-1},$$

so that the formula holds for $m=k+1$, and so for all values of m $\leqslant n$.

Notice that the derivative of a polynomial is a polynomial and the derivative of a rational function (ratio of two polynomials) is a rational function.

(ii) *Trigonometrical functions*

We regard $\sin\theta$ as a function of the angle θ measured in radians. Recall that the radian measure of an angle is the length[1] of the arc, of a circle of unit radius, subtended by the angle; then $\frac{\pi}{2}$ radians$=90°$.

For $0<\theta<\frac{\pi}{2}$, $\sin\theta$ is defined by the usual rule. This is equivalent to saying that $\sin\theta=y$, where (x,y) are the co-ordinates of the point P such that OP is of unit length and

---

[1] There is a theoretical difficulty about the concept of 'length of arc' into which we will not enter.

makes an angle θ with the positive direction of the x-axis. We extend the definition to any angle θ satisfying $-\pi < \theta \leqslant \pi$ by putting $\sin \theta = y$ as above, and finally to arbitrary θ by the rule

$$\sin (\theta + 2\pi) = \sin \theta. \qquad (2.10)$$

Then $\cos \theta$ may be defined by

$$\cos \theta = \sin \left(\frac{\pi}{2} - \theta \right), \qquad (2.11)$$

or directly, and $\tan \theta$ by

$$\tan \theta = \frac{\sin \theta}{\cos \theta};$$

notice that $\tan \theta$ takes the (conventional) values $\pm \infty$ when $\theta = \pm \dfrac{\pi}{2}$. Finally, we have

$$\operatorname{cosec} \theta = 1/\sin \theta, \ \sec \theta = 1/\cos \theta, \ \cot \theta = 1/\tan \theta.$$

It is clear that the rules of the previous section will enable us to differentiate any trigonometrical function, once we know $\dfrac{d}{d\theta} \sin \theta$.

Formula 2.2. $\dfrac{d}{d\theta} \sin \theta = \cos \theta.$

We seek $\qquad \lim\limits_{h \to 0} \dfrac{\sin(\theta + h) - \sin \theta}{h}.$

Now $\sin (\theta + h) - \sin \theta = 2 \sin \dfrac{h}{2} \cos \left(\theta + \dfrac{h}{2} \right)$. Thus, replacing $\dfrac{h}{2}$ by k, we have $\lim\limits_{h \to 0} \dfrac{\sin (\theta + h) - \sin \theta}{h} = \lim\limits_{k \to 0} \dfrac{\sin k}{k} . \cos (\theta + k)$. Now, by continuity, $\lim\limits_{k \to 0} \cos (\theta + k) = \cos \theta$. Thus it remains to establish the fundamental result, which we state as a lemma.[1]

Lemma 2.1. $\lim\limits_{k \to 0} \dfrac{\sin k}{k} = 1.$

[1] A lemma is a result needed in the proof of another result and introduced just for that purpose.

Since $\sin(-k) = -\sin k$, it is sufficient to consider k positive; certainly we may take $k < \dfrac{\pi}{2}$. In Fig. 5, let OP meet the tangent at X in T. Then the area of the triangle POX is $\frac{1}{2}\sin k$, that of the sector[1] POX is $\frac{1}{2}k$, and that of the triangle TOX is $\frac{1}{2}\tan k$. Thus

$$\sin k < k < \tan k,$$

whence $\qquad \cos k < \dfrac{\sin k}{k} < 1.$

Fig. 5.—$\Delta POX <$ sector $POX < \Delta TOX$, hence $\sin k < k < \tan k$.

Now as $k \to 0$, $\cos k \to 1$. Since $\dfrac{\sin k}{k}$ is sandwiched between $\cos k$ and 1, it is obvious that it, too, must tend to 1. This proves the lemma, and hence Formula 2.2.

Formula 2.3. $\dfrac{d}{d\theta}\cos\theta = -\sin\theta.$

Put $\theta = \dfrac{\pi}{2} - \phi$; then if $y = \cos\theta$ we have $y = \sin\phi$, $\dfrac{dy}{d\phi} = \cos\phi$, $\dfrac{d\phi}{d\theta} = -1$, so that

$$\frac{dy}{d\theta} = -\cos\phi = -\sin\theta.$$

Formula 2.4. $\dfrac{d}{d\theta}\tan\theta = \sec^2\theta.$

For
$$\frac{d}{d\theta}\tan\theta = \frac{d}{d\theta}\frac{\sin\theta}{\cos\theta} = \frac{\cos\theta \cdot \cos\theta - \sin\theta(-\sin\theta)}{\cos^2\theta} = \frac{\cos^2\theta + \sin^2\theta}{\cos^2\theta}$$
$$= \frac{1}{\cos^2\theta} = \sec^2\theta.$$

[1] There are also difficulties about the concept of area of regions bounded by curves (see footnote on p. 23); so this argument should only be regarded as the outline of a full rigorous proof.

We defer the derivatives of the remaining trigonometrical functions to the exercises at the end of the chapter, and turn to the inverse trigonometrical functions. The function $y = \sin x$ is a one–one function from the interval $-\dfrac{\pi}{2} \leqslant x < \dfrac{\pi}{2}$ to the interval $-1 \leqslant y \leqslant 1$, and so has an inverse which we write $x = \sin^{-1} y$ $\left(\text{note that } \sin^{-1} y \text{ does } not \text{ mean } \dfrac{1}{\sin y}\right)$ and which we may differentiate at any interior point of the interval $-1 \leqslant y \leqslant 1$. We obtain

$$\frac{dx}{dy} = \frac{1}{\cos x} = \frac{1}{\sqrt{(1-y^2)}},$$

since $\cos x$ is positive in the first and fourth quadrants. We have therefore proved

Formula 2.5. *If* $y = \sin^{-1} x$, $-1 < x < 1$, *then* $\dfrac{dy}{dx} = \dfrac{1}{\sqrt{(1-x^2)}}$.

We repeat for emphasis that $\sin^{-1} x$ takes values between $-\dfrac{\pi}{2}$ and $\dfrac{\pi}{2}$. Similarly we prove, with the obvious meaning for $\cos^{-1} x$,

Formula 2.6. *If* $y = \cos^{-1} x$, $-1 < x < 1$, *then* $\dfrac{dy}{dx} = -\dfrac{1}{\sqrt{(1-x^2)}}$.

Here y takes values between 0 and π. The reader will be able to supply the proof of this formula; it may also be obtained from the previous formula and the relation

$$\sin^{-1} x + \cos^{-1} x = \frac{\pi}{2}.$$

We also have

Formula 2.7. *If* $y = \tan^{-1} x$, *then* $\dfrac{dy}{dx} = \dfrac{1}{1+x^2}$.

Here there is no restriction on x, since the function tan takes all values; but y takes values between $-\dfrac{\pi}{2}$ and $\dfrac{\pi}{2}$.

We see in the ranges of y in Formulae 2.5 and 2.7 the force of measuring angles from $-\pi$ to π.

(iii) *Exponential and logarithmic functions*

The reader will probably be familiar with the exponential function, written exp x or e^x. It may be defined in several ways; we select two, namely

Definition 2.5(a). exp x is the sum of the series

$$1+x+\frac{x^2}{2!}+ \ldots +\frac{x^n}{n!}+ \ldots$$

Definition 2.5(b). exp x is the unique function $f(x)$ satisfying $f'(x)=f(x)$, $f(0)=1$.

It will follow from Theorem 3.4 in the next chapter that a function $f(x)$ is uniquely determined by the properties $f'(x)=f(x)$, $f(0)=1$. Here we observe that exp x, defined by 2.5(a), does satisfy $f'(x)=f(x)$, $f(0)=1$; the verification of the former property requires the fact that we are entitled to differentiate a power series term by term.

We may justify the notation e^x as follows. Consider Definition 2.5(b). Since $\dfrac{d}{dx}$ exp $x=$exp x, it follows from Theorem 2.3 that

$$\frac{d}{dx}(\exp x.\exp(a-x))=\exp x(-\exp(a-x))$$

$$+\exp x.\exp(a-x)=0.$$

Thus, assuming Theorem 3.4,

$$\exp x.\exp(a-x)=c.$$

Putting $x=0$, we see that $c=$exp a, so that

$$\exp x.\exp(a-x)=\exp a$$

for all x. In other words, putting $z=x+y$,

$$\exp x.\exp y=\exp(x+y). \tag{2.12}$$

(2.12) is proved from Definition 2.5(a) in the book by J. A. Green in this series (see footnote 1, p. 28). In particular, (2.12) implies exp $n=(\exp 1)^n$, if n is a positive integer. From this we may deduce that exp $\dfrac{p}{q}=(\exp 1)^{\frac{p}{q}}$ for any rational number $\dfrac{p}{q}$.

In proving this we may suppose q positive. Then

$$\left(\exp\frac{1}{q}\right)^q = \exp 1,$$

from (2.12). We next observe that exp x is *always positive*; this follows from Definition 2.5(a) if $x > 0$ and follows for negative x from the relation

$$\exp x \,.\, \exp(-x) = 1,$$

a special case of (2.12). It follows from this that

$$\exp\frac{1}{q} = (\exp 1)^{\frac{1}{q}}.$$

Now, if p is positive, we immediately infer that

$$\exp\frac{p}{q} = \left(\exp\frac{1}{q}\right)^p = \left((\exp 1)^{\frac{1}{q}}\right)^p = (\exp 1)^{\frac{p}{q}},$$

and if p is negative we infer the result by taking reciprocals. It is customary to write e for exp 1, so that

$$\exp x = e^x, \tag{2.13}$$

if x is a rational number; the number e is approximately $2 \cdot 718$. The question arises as to whether (2.13) holds for all x; the only difficulty here is to give a meaning to the expression e^x when x is not a rational number. The solution of this difficulty is again in terms of the concept of limit. If a is any real number, we define a^x to be the limit,[1] as the rational numbers x_n tend to x, of a^{x_n}. Then it follows from the continuity of exp x that, with this definition of e^x, (2.13) holds for all x, and so we may use the notation e^x for exp x. Thus we have the formula

Formula 2.8. *If* $y = e^x$, *then* $\dfrac{dy}{dx} = e^x$.

We remark that we may define exp x by the equation (2.12), together with the assumption of continuity and the value of exp 1.

We now consider the inverse function. Since $y = e^x$ is a one–one function of the whole x-axis on the positive part of the

[1] See J. A. Green, *Sequences and Series*, Chapter 1, § 4, in this series; (x_n) is *any* sequence of rationals tending to x.

y-axis, there is an inverse function which is written $x=\log_e y$, the logarithm of y to base e, defined for all positive values of y. We will write log for $\log_e$; we then have

Formula 2.9. *If* $y=\log x$, *then* $\dfrac{dy}{dx}=\dfrac{1}{x}$.

For $x=e^y$, $\dfrac{dx}{dy}=e^y$, $\dfrac{dy}{dx}=\dfrac{1}{e^y}=\dfrac{1}{x}$.

It follows easily from (2.12) that

$$\log x+\log y=\log\ (xy) \tag{2.14}$$

From this we deduce that $\log\ (x^m)=m\log x$, if m is a rational number, and hence, by the continuity of each side as a function of m, that

$$\log\ (x^m)=m\log x \tag{2.15}$$

for all real m and positive x; but this implies that

$$x^m=e^{m\ \log x} \tag{2.16}$$

We immediately deduce

Formula 2.10. *If* $y=a^x$, *then* $\dfrac{dy}{dx}=a^x\log a$.

Taking the inverse function, we have

Formula 2.11. *If* $y=\log_a x$, *then* $\dfrac{dy}{dx}=\dfrac{1}{x\log a}$.

We close this subsection by remarking that, with our definition of x^n for arbitrary (real) n, Formula 2.1 continues to hold; for if $y=x^n$, then $y=e^{n\ \log x}=e^z$, where $z=n\log x$. Thus

$$\frac{dy}{dx}=\frac{dy}{dz}\cdot\frac{dz}{dx}=e^z\cdot\frac{n}{x}=x^n\cdot\frac{n}{x}=nx^{n-1}.$$

Example 2.8. If $y=x^x$, then $\dfrac{dy}{dx}=x^x(1+\log x)$.

We have $\log y=x\log x$, whence, differentiating,

$$\frac{1}{y}\frac{dy}{dx}=1+\log x.$$

Thus $\dfrac{dy}{dx}=y(1+\log x)=x^x(1+\log x)$.

(iv) *Hyperbolic functions*

The hyperbolic functions are defined by

$$\cosh x = \frac{e^x + e^{-x}}{2},$$

$$\sinh x = \frac{e^x - e^{-x}}{2},$$

$$\tanh x = \frac{\sinh x}{\cosh x}$$

sech $x = 1/\cosh x$, cosech $x = 1/\sinh x$, coth $x = 1/\tanh x$.

Then Formula 2.8 yields

Formula 2.12. $\dfrac{d}{dx} \cosh x = \sinh x$, $\dfrac{d}{dx} \sinh x = \cosh x$,

$$\frac{d}{dx} \tanh x = \text{sech}^2 x.$$

The first two are obvious; the third follows from Theorem 2.4 and the identity

$$\cosh^2 x - \sinh^2 x = 1 \qquad (2.17)$$

We leave the derivatives of the remaining hyperbolic functions as exercises, and turn our attention to the inverse hyperbolic functions. Let $y = \cosh x$, so that y is positive; indeed $y \geqslant 1$. Then

$$e^x + e^{-x} = 2y,$$

$$e^{2x} - 2y \cdot e^x + 1 = 0,$$

whence $\qquad e^x = y \pm \sqrt{(y^2 - 1)}$,

so that $\qquad x = \log (y \pm \sqrt{(y^2 - 1)})$.

Since $y - \sqrt{(y^2-1)} = \dfrac{1}{y + \sqrt{(y^2-1)}}$ and $\log \dfrac{1}{a} = -\log a$, we may

write the solution as

$$x = \pm \log (y + \sqrt{(y^2 - 1)}).$$

Thus $y = \cosh x$ is a one–one function from the positive x-axis to $y \geqslant 1$ with inverse

$$x = \log (y + \sqrt{(y^2 - 1)}) \qquad (2.18)$$

We easily verify, using $\cosh^{-1}$ for the inverse function, given by (2.18),

Formula 2.13. *If* $y = \cosh^{-1} x$, *then* $\dfrac{dy}{dx} = \dfrac{1}{\sqrt{(x^2 - 1)}}$

Similarly if $y = \sinh x$, then

$$e^{2x} - 2y \cdot e^x - 1 = 0,$$

whence $\qquad\qquad e^x = y \pm \sqrt{(y^2 + 1)};$

but here the positive sign must be taken since e^x is positive, so that

$$x = \log(y + \sqrt{(y^2 + 1)}) \qquad\qquad (2.19)$$

Thus $y = \sinh x$ is a one–one function from the whole x-axis to the whole y-axis, with inverse $\sinh^{-1} y = \log(y + \sqrt{(y^2 + 1)})$. We easily verify

Formula 2.14. *If* $y = \sinh^{-1} x$, *then* $\dfrac{dy}{dx} = \dfrac{1}{\sqrt{(x^2 + 1)}}$

Now let $\quad y = \tanh x = \dfrac{e^x - e^{-x}}{e^x + e^{-x}} = \dfrac{e^{2x} - 1}{e^{2x} + 1};\quad$ then $\quad e^{2x} = \dfrac{1 + y}{1 - y},\quad$ so that

$$x = \tfrac{1}{2} \log \frac{1 + y}{1 - y} = \tfrac{1}{2} (\log(1 + y) - \log(1 - y)).$$

Thus, interchanging x and y, $\tanh^{-1} x = \tfrac{1}{2} \log \dfrac{1 + x}{1 - x}$, so that we may verify directly

Formula 2.15. *If* $y = \tanh^{-1} x$, *then* $\dfrac{dy}{dx} = \dfrac{1}{1 - x^2}$

Notice that $y = \tanh^{-1} x$ is a function from the interval $-1 < x < 1$ to the whole y-axis.

Example 2.9. Differentiate $\tanh^{-1}(\sin x)$.

We apply Theorem 2.5 to obtain

$$\frac{d}{dx}(\tanh^{-1}(\sin x)) = \frac{\cos x}{1 - \sin^2 x} = \frac{\cos x}{\cos^2 x} = \sec x.$$

The formulae given in this section should be adequate for

most of the problems of differentiation met in practice, especially if supplemented by the rules given in the previous section. However, the reader should beware of supposing this list, or any other, to be exhaustive; it may very well happen that a particular differential coefficient can only be worked out 'from first principles', i.e., direct from Definition 2.3. Let us take an example.

Example 2.10. Differentiate[1] $x|x|$.

If we attempt to use the product rule of Theorem 2.3 we run into the difficulty that $|x|$ has no differential coefficient at the origin. From first principles we observe that, if $f(x)=x\,|x|$, then $f'(0)= \lim_{x\to 0} \dfrac{x|x|}{x}=0$. Since $f(x)=x^2$, when $x>0$ and $f(x)=-x^2$, $x<0$, we infer that $f'(x)=2|x|$.

EXERCISES ON CHAPTER II

Differentiate:—

1. x^3+3x^2-7.
2. $5x^6-6x^5$.
3. $\frac{1}{2}x^4+9x^3+2$.
4. $\dfrac{x+1}{x^2+1}$.
5. $\dfrac{x^{\frac{1}{2}}+3x^2}{3x^{\frac{1}{2}}+1}$.
6. $\sin^2 x$.
7. $\cos 3x$.
8. $\tan^{-1}(2x+1)-\sin x^2$.
9. $x\sin^{-1} x$.
10. $\dfrac{\cos^{-1} 2x}{1-x}$.
11. e^{ax+b}.
12. e^{e^x}.
13. $e^{1+\log x}$.
14. $\log \sin x$.
15. $\log \log x$.
16. x^{x^x}.
17. $\cosh(-5x)$.
18. $\log \cosh x$.
19. $\cosh \log x$.
20. $f(x)=x^2 \sin \dfrac{1}{x}$, $x\neq 0$, $f(0)=0$.

21. What is the tangent to the curve $xy=c^2$ at the point with x-coordinate ct?
22. A curve is given parametrically by $x=x(t)$, $y=y(t)$. What is the equation of the tangent at t_0?

---

[1] $|x|$ stands, as usual, for the absolute value of x, i.e. $|x|=x, x\geqslant 0$, $|x|=-x$, $x<0$.

23. A particle is moving under the law $s = \dfrac{a^2}{g} \log \cosh \dfrac{gt}{a}$. Prove that its acceleration and velocity are related by the formula $\dfrac{d^2s}{dt^2} = g - k\left(\dfrac{ds}{dt}\right)^2$, where $k = \dfrac{g}{a^2}$.

24. If $q(x) = f(x)/g(x)$, find D^2q.

25. Generalize Theorem 2.3 to the product of n factors.

26. Prove that, given any polynomial $f(x)$, there is a polynomial $g(x)$ with $g'(x) = f(x)$. Is a similar statement true for rational functions?

27. $y = \sin x$ is a one–one function from $\dfrac{\pi}{2} \leqslant x \leqslant \dfrac{3\pi}{2}$ to $-1 \leqslant y \leqslant 1$. What is the inverse? What is the derivative of the inverse?

28. $y = \cos x$ is a one–one function from $-\pi \leqslant x \leqslant 0$ to $-1 \leqslant y \leqslant 1$. What is the inverse? What is the derivative of the inverse?

29. Differentiate $\sec x$, $\operatorname{cosec} x$, $\cot x$, $\operatorname{sech} x$, $\operatorname{cosech} x$, $\coth x$.

30. Find expressions for $\operatorname{sech}^{-1} x (0 < x \leqslant 1)$, $\operatorname{cosech}^{-1} x$, $\coth^{-1} x$ $(|x| > 1)$, and find their derivatives.

CHAPTER THREE

Maxima and Minima and Taylor's Theorem

I. MEAN VALUE THEOREM

WE first state the theorem

Theorem 3.1. (*Mean Value Theorem*) *Let $f(x)$ be differentiable at all points between $x=a$ and $x=a+h$. Then there exists a real number θ satisfying $0<\theta<1$ such that*

$$f(a+h)=f(a)+hf'(a+\theta h). \tag{3.1}$$

Let us consider this theorem geometrically. The expression $\dfrac{f(a+h)-f(a)}{h}$ is the gradient of the chord joining the points on the curve $y=f(x)$ with x-coordinates a and $a+h$. Now $a+\theta h$ is some number between a and $a+h$, so that $f'(a+\theta h)$ is the gradient of the tangent to the curve at the point whose x-coordinate is $a+\theta h$. Thus the theorem asserts that, given any two points P,R on the curve there is a point Q between P and R such that the tangent at Q is parallel to the chord PR.

Next, let us consider the theorem numerically. (3.1) implies

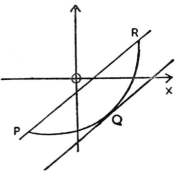

FIG. 6.—Mean Value Theorem (Chord PR is parallel to tangent at Q).

that the increase (or decrease) in $f(x)$ between $x=a$ and $x=a+h$ is approximately proportional to h; the factor of proportionality, however, instead of being constant, actually varies with h, but the variation is small if h is small, when the factor is approximately $f'(a)$. Actually some such statement could already be made from the very definition of $f'(a)$; the added interest provided by the mean value theorem is that the factor of proportionality is always given by the value of $f'(x)$ at some point between $x=a$ and $x=a+h$. This enables us in particular cases to estimate the accuracy of the *linear* approximation

$$f(a)+(x-a)f'(a)$$

to the function $f(x)$ near $x=a$; that is, how rapidly the curve diverges from the tangent at $x=a$. (Recall that a *linear* function of x is a polynomial in x of the first degree.)

We now prove the theorem.[1] We first need a result which is really a special case of theorem 3.1 (henceforth referred to as MVT).

Theorem 3.2 (*Rolle's Theorem*) *Let $f(x)$ be a differentiable function of x. If $f(b)=f(a)$, then there exists a point c, between a and b, such that $f'(c)=0$.*

We see from Fig. 6 that MVT is just Rolle's Theorem 'turned on its side'. To prove Rolle's theorem, we may suppose $b>a$; then c will satisfy $a<c<b$. We may also suppose $f(b)=f(a)=0$, otherwise we consider the function $g(x)=f(x)-f(a)$. Then $g(a)=g(b)=0$ and $g'(x)=f'(x)$. Next we may suppose that $f(x)$ is not identically zero in $a\leqslant x\leqslant b$; for if it were, any c satisfying $a<c<b$ would do. Finally we may suppose that $f(x)$ takes positive values in $a<c<b$; for if not it would take negative values so that the function $g(x)=-f(x)$ would take positive values. Moreover, if we suppose the theorem proved for functions taking positive values, there would be a number c, $a<c<b$, such that $g'(c)=0$. But then $f'(c)=-g'(c)=0$, so that the theorem would hold for $f(x)$. Thus it remains to prove the theorem when $f(x)$ takes positive values.

[1] The reader should always try to understand the proof of a theorem, but he should not be required to memorize a proof.

It is obvious from a picture that we would expect the derivative to vanish at a maximum or minimum; now we have the theorem that a continuous function takes a maximum and minimum value in any interval $a \leqslant x \leqslant b$. Now the maximum value cannot be at a or b since $f(x)$ is zero there and assumes positive values. Thus the maximum is at some point c such that $a < c < b$. We prove that $f'(c) = 0$.

The argument is by reductio ad absurdum; that is, we suppose our statement false and obtain a contradiction. Suppose then that $f'(c) > 0$. Since $f'(c) = \lim_{h \to 0} \dfrac{f(c+h) - f(c)}{h}$, it follows that $\dfrac{f(c+h) - f(c)}{h} > 0$ for h sufficiently small; but then, if $h > 0$, this implies that $f(c+h) > f(c)$, so that $f(x)$ does not have a maximum at $x = c$. Now suppose $f'(c) < 0$; it then follows that $\dfrac{f(c+h) - f(c)}{h} < 0$ for h sufficiently small. Thus, if $h < 0$, $f(c+h) > f(c)$, so that again $f(x)$ does not have a maximum at $x = c$, and we are forced to conclude, as required by the theorem, that $f'(c) = 0$.

Notice that it is essential for the validity of the conclusion of Rolle's Theorem that we assume that $f(x)$ is differentiable at every point between a and b. Thus, if we consider the function $y = \tan x$, then $\tan 0 = \tan \pi$, but $\sec^2 x$ never vanishes. There is no contradiction here because the function $\tan x$ is not defined, let alone differentiable, at $x = \dfrac{\pi}{2}$.

Before completing the proof of MVT, we take advantage of the proof of Rolle's Theorem to deduce a vitally important consequence. Let us generalize the meaning of the words 'maximum' and 'minimum' to give them a 'local' meaning; that is to say, we will call $f(c)$ a *maximum* of $f(x)$ if there is some interval $a \leqslant x \leqslant b$, containing c in its interior, in which $f(x)$ never exceeds $f(c)$—and similarly for a *minimum*. Then the proof of Rolle's Theorem contains the following conclusion.

Theorem 3.3. *If $f(x)$ has a maximum or minimum at $x = c$, then* $f'(c) = 0$.

Now, finally, we prove MVT. As we have remarked, it is obvious geometrically from Rolle's Theorem. Algebraically, we proceed by considering the function

$$F(x)=f(x)-f(a)-\frac{x-a}{h}(f(a+h)-f(a)) \qquad (3.2)$$

Then, obviously, $F(a)=F(a+h)=0$, so that, by Rolle's Theorem, there exists $c=a+\theta h$, $0<\theta<1$, such that $F'(a+\theta h)=0$; but $F'(x)=f'(x)-\dfrac{f(a+h)-f(a)}{h}$. Thus

$$\frac{f(a+h)-f(a)}{h}=f'(a+\theta h), \text{ or}$$

$$f(a+h)=f(a)+hf'(a+\theta h).$$

Corollary 3.1. *If $f'(x)=0$, identically, then $f(x)$ is constant.*

We have to prove that, for any two points a,b, $f(a)=f(b)$. Now

$$f(b)=f(a)+(b-a)f'(c), \text{ for some } c \text{ between } a \text{ and } b;$$

but $\qquad f'(c)=0$, so that $f(b)=f(a)$.

This corollary is 'obvious' and is often tacitly assumed in elementary treatises on the calculus; but it is always preferable to have a proof of even the most obvious facts.[1] The corollary itself entails, and is equivalent to, the following fundamental theorem.

Theorem 3.4. *$f(x)$, $g(x)$ have the same derivatives if and only if they differ by a constant.*

For if $f(x)=g(x)+c$, then $f'(x)=g'(x)$. Conversely, if $f'(x)=g'(x)$ and $h(x)=f(x)-g(x)$, then $h'(x)=0$, so that, by Corollary 3.1, $h(x)$ is constant.

Theorem 3.4 is really a theorem of the integral calculus, but its fundamental nature warrants its inclusion here. It shows that a function is completely determined by its derivative and its value at one point; for the value at the point determines the arbitrary constant. Thus

Example 3.1. Find the function whose derivative is x and whose value for $x=2$ is 5.

[1] The existence of witches used to be 'obvious'.

Now, certainly the derivative of $\frac{1}{2}x^2$ is x. Thus the given function is of the form $\frac{1}{2}x^2 + c$. We require that $\frac{1}{2}x^2 + c = 5$ when $x = 2$; so $2 + c = 5$, $c = 3$, and the required function is $\frac{1}{2}x^2 + 3$.

Example 3.2. A unique function (the exponential function) is determined by the properties $f'(x) = f(x)$, $f(0) = 1$.

Define exp x by Definition 2.5(a). Then this is a function $f(x)$ satisfying $f'(x) = f(x)$, $f(0) = 1$. Moreover $f(x)$ $(= \exp x)$ never vanishes. Let $g(x)$ by any other function satisfying $g'(x) = g(x)$. Now $\dfrac{d}{dx}\left(\dfrac{g(x)}{f(x)}\right) = \dfrac{f(x)g'(x) - g(x)f'(x)}{(f(x))^2} = 0$. Thus, by Corollary 3.1, $g(x) = cf(x)$, for some constant c. Thus, if also $g(0) = 1$, we have $c = 1$, and $g(x) = f(x)$.

Example 3.3. Find c, such that $f(b) = f(a) + (b - a)f'(c)$, when $f(x) = \tan x$, $a = 0$, $b = \dfrac{\pi}{4}$.

Then $f'(x) = \sec^2 x$, so that $1 = \dfrac{\pi}{4}\sec^2 c$, $\cos c = \dfrac{\sqrt{\pi}}{2}$, whence $c = 27° \ 34'$, approximately.

Rolle's Theorem is important in the study of the number of zeros of a polynomial. For let $f(x)$ be a polynomial of degree n. Then $f'(x)$ is a polynomial of degree $(n-1)$, and has a zero between any two zeros of $f(x)$, by Rolle's Theorem. Here we are, of course, restricting attention to *real* zeros of $f(x)$; all quantities considered in this book are real.

Let us also note

Theorem 3.5. *If $(x-a)^m$ is a factor of the polynomial $f(x)$, then $(x-a)^{m-1}$ is a factor of $f'(x)$.* (We say that $(x-a)$ is an m-fold factor of $f(x)$, or that a is an m-fold zero of $f(x)$, if $(x-a)^m$ is a factor of $f(x)$ but $(x-a)^{m+1}$ is not a factor of $f(x)$.)

For $f(x) = (x-a)^m g(x)$, so that

$$f'(x) = (x-a)^m g'(x) + m(x-a)^{m-1}g(x).$$

It follows, from this and the previous remark, that if we count an m-fold zero m times, then we have

Theorem 3.6. *If $f(x)$ is a polynomial with q zeros, then $f'(x)$ is a polynomial with at least $(q-1)$ zeros.*

38

Example 3.4. Prove that the cubic equation

$$ax^3 + bx^2 + cx + d = 0$$

has only one root if $b^2 < 3ac$.

Now every cubic equation has at least one root (since a cubic polynomial always changes sign). If $f(x) = ax^3 + bx^2 + cx + d$, then $f'(x) = 3ax^2 + 2bx + c$. Then $f'(x)$ has no zeros if $b^2 < 3ac$. Thus, if $b^2 < 3ac$, the equation has only one root, by Theorem 3.6.

Example 3.5. The equation $x^4 - 3x^3 - 13x^2 + 51x - 36 = 0$ has a repeated root. Solve the equation.

Such a root is also a root of $4x^3 - 9x^2 - 26x + 51 = 0$. We find that the H.C.F. of $x^4 - 3x^3 - 13x^2 + 51x - 36$ and

$$4x^3 - 9x^2 - 26x + 51$$

is $(x - 3)$. Thus we verify that $x - 3$ is a repeated factor of $x^4 - 3x^3 - 13x^2 + 51x - 36$. Dividing by $x^2 - 6x + 9$, we get a quotient $x^2 + 3x - 4$. Now $x^2 + 3x - 4 = 0$ if $x = -4$ or 1. Thus the roots of the given equation are 3, -4, and 1. Of course, this problem could have been solved by experimenting with factors of 36, the constant term.

Before proceeding to Taylor's Theorem, we state one further consequence of MVT and prove a variant of MVT.

Theorem 3.7. *Suppose $f'(x)$ is positive (negative) for $a < x < b$. Then $f(x)$ is increasing (decreasing) in $a \leqslant x \leqslant b$.*

For choose a_1, b_1 with $a \leqslant a_1 < b_1 \leqslant b$. Then

$$f(b_1) = f(a_1) + (b_1 - a_1)f'(c_1),$$

where $a_1 < c_1 < b_1$. But then $f'(c_1) > 0$, by hypothesis, so that $f(b_1) > f(a_1)$. A similar argument holds when $f'(x)$ is negative, so that the proof is complete.

Now the proof of MVT for $f(x)$ consisted in applying Rolle's Theorem to a certain function $F(x)$ (see (3.2)). Now let $g(x)$ be another differentiable function whose derivative does not vanish between a and $a + h$, and consider

$$F_1(x) = f(x) - f(a) - \frac{g(x) - g(a)}{g(a+h) - g(a)}(f(a+h) - f(a)).$$

Notice that, by Rolle's Theorem, $g(a+h)-g(a)\neq 0$, since otherwise $g'(x)$ would vanish between a and $a+h$. Then

$$F_1(a)=F_1(a+h)=0,$$

so that, for some θ such that $0<\theta<1$,

$$0=f'(a+\theta h)-g'(a+\theta h)\frac{(f(a+h)-f(a))}{g(a+h)-g(a)}.$$

We have proved

Theorem 3.8. (*Cauchy Mean Value Theorem*) *Under the above hypothesis on* $g(x)$,

$$\frac{f(a+h)-f(a)}{g(a+h)-g(a)}=\frac{f'(a+\theta h)}{g'(a+\theta h)}, \text{ for some } \theta \text{ satisfying } 0<\theta<1.$$

Suppose $f(a)=g(a)=0$. Then $\lim\limits_{x\to a}\dfrac{f(x)}{g(x)}$, if it exists, cannot be obtained by substituting a for x in $\dfrac{f(x)}{g(x)}$. However, suppose further that $\lim\limits_{x\to a}\dfrac{f'(x)}{g'(x)}$ exists and equals l. Since

$$\frac{f(a+h)}{g(a+h)} = \frac{f'(a+\theta h)}{g'(a+\theta h)},$$

and the right-hand side can be brought as near to l as we like by taking h sufficiently small, so can the left-hand side. Thus we have proved

Theorem 3.9. *Suppose* $f(a)=g(a)=0$ *and* $\dfrac{f'(x)}{g'(x)}\to l$ *as* $x\to a$.

Then $\qquad\qquad \dfrac{f(x)}{g(x)}\to l \text{ as } x\to a.$

Example 3.6. Find $\lim\limits_{x\to 0}\dfrac{\tan^{-1}x}{\sin^{-1}x}$.

Now $\tan^{-1}0=0$, $\sin^{-1}0=0$. Thus

$$\lim_{x\to 0}\frac{\tan^{-1}x}{\sin^{-1}x}=\lim_{x\to 0}\frac{\sqrt{(1-x^2)}}{1+x^2},$$

if the latter exists; but $\lim\limits_{x\to 0}\dfrac{\sqrt{(1-x^2)}}{1+x^2}=1$, so that $\lim\limits_{x\to 0}\dfrac{\tan^{-1}x}{\sin^{-1}x}=1$.

2. TAYLOR'S THEOREM

As remarked, we may regard MVT as giving a linear approximation to a function $f(x)$ near a point $x=a$. We would expect that if we allowed a quadratic term in $(x-a)$ we would be able to approximate even more closely to $f(x)$ and so on. This is in fact the case; the final story is contained in the following theorem.

Theorem 3.10. (*Taylor's Theorem*)

$$(b)=f(a)+(b-a)f'(a)+\frac{(b-a)^2}{2!}f''(a)+\ \ldots$$
$$+\frac{(b-a)^{n-1}}{(n-1)!}f^{(n-1)}(a)+\frac{(b-a)^n}{n!}f^{(n)}(c).$$

where c lies between a and b.

Of course, we assume that all the derivatives exist. The theorem is proved by a trick; we consider the function

$$F(x)=f(b)-f(x)-(b-x)f'(x)$$
$$-\frac{(b-x)^2}{2!}f''(x)-\ \ldots\ -\frac{(b-x)^{n-1}}{(n-1)!}f^{(n-1)}(x).$$

Then $F(b)=0$; thus if $G(x)=F(x)-\frac{(b-x)^n}{(b-a)^n}F(a)$, we have

$G(a)=G(b)=0$. It follows from MVT that for some c between

a and b, $G'(c)=0$. But $G'(x)=F'(x)+\frac{n(b-x)^{n-1}}{(b-a)^n}F(a)$, whence

$$F'(c)+\frac{n(b-c)^{n-1}}{(b-a)^n}F(a)=0.$$

Now $\quad F'(x)=\ -f'(x)+f'(x)-(b-x)f''(x)+\ \ldots$
$$+\frac{(b-x)^{n-2}}{(n-2)!}f^{(n-1)}(x)-\frac{(b-x)^{n-1}}{(n-1)!}f^{(n)}(x)$$
$$=\ -\frac{(b-x)^{n-1}}{(n-1)!}f^{(n)}(x).$$

Thus $-\dfrac{(b-c)^{n-1}}{(n-1)!}f^{(n)}(c)+\dfrac{n(b-c)^{n-1}}{(b-a)^n}F(a)=$ o. Since $b-c\neq$ o, we have

$$F(a)=\frac{(b-a)^n}{n!}f^{(n)}(c).$$

Reference to the definition of $F(x)$ completes the proof.

Taylor's Theorem plays a fundamental role, as we shall see; we may express its conclusions roughly by saying that we may approximate to $f(x)$ near a by the polynomial, of degree n in $(x-a)$,

$$f(a)+(x-a)f'(a)+\frac{(x-a)^2}{2!}f''(a)+ \ldots +\frac{(x-a)^n}{n!}f^{(n)}(a) \qquad (3.3)$$

To emphasize this aspect, let us suppose that we actually start with a polynomial $f(x)$ of degree n. Certainly all derivatives of order higher than n vanish. Indeed, in this case, we may show that $f(x)$ is precisely equal to the expression (3.3). For certainly any such polynomial $f(x)$ of degree n may be expressed as

$$f(x)=c_0+c_1(x-a)+\frac{c_2}{2!}(x-a)^2+ \ldots +\frac{c_n}{n!}(x-a)^n; \qquad (3.4)$$

we simply express $f(a+y)$ as a polynomial in y, say $d_0+d_1y+ \ldots +d_ny^n$, and then $c_r=r!d_r$, $r=$ o,1, ..., n. Differentiating r times, we have

$$f^{(r)}(x)=c_r+c_{r+1}(x-a)+ \ldots +\frac{c_n}{(n-r)!}(x-a)^{n-r},$$

so that, putting $x=a$, $f^{(r)}(a)=c_r$ as required.

Moreover we may show that (3.3) is the best possible approximation to $f(x)$ (now an arbitrary differentiable function) near a by a polynomial of degree n. For we know that the difference is expressible as

$$\frac{(x-a)^{n+1}}{(n+1)!}f^{(n+1)}(c),$$

where c lies between x and a. If we took any other polynomial, $p(x)$, of degree n, then $f(x)-p(x)$ would be expressible as

$k(x-a)^r+$ terms involving higher powers of $x-a$, where $k\neq0$ and $r\leqslant n$. Now, if x is near to a, then $(x-a)^m$ decreases as m increases, and this shows that, for x sufficiently near to a,

$$|f(x)-p(x)|>\left|\frac{(x-a)^{n+1}}{(n+1)!}f^{(n+1)}(c)\right|.$$

Example 3.7. Approximate to $\sin x$ by a polynomial in x of degree $(2n+1)$.

Let $f(x)=\sin x$; then $f^{(4m)}(x)=\sin x$, $f^{(4m+1)}(x)=\cos x$, $f^{(4m+2)}(x)=-\sin x, f^{(4m+3)}(x)=-\cos x$.
The approximation is

$$f(0)+f'(0)x+\frac{f''(0)}{2!}x^2+\dots+\frac{f^{(2n)}(0)}{(2n)!}x^{2n}+\frac{f^{(2n+1)}(0)}{(2n+1)!}x^{2n+1}.$$

Now $f^{(2m)}(0)=0$ and $f^{2m+1}(0)=(-1)^m$. Thus the required approximation is

$$x-\frac{x^3}{3!}+\frac{x^5}{5!}-\dots+(-1)^n\frac{x^{2n+1}}{(2n+1)!}.$$

Example 3.8. Approximate to $\log(1+x)$ by a polynomial in x of degree n.

Let $f(x)=\log(1+x)$. Then

$$f'(x)=\frac{1}{1+x}, f''(x)=-\frac{\cdot 1}{(1+x)^2}, \dots, f^{(n)}(x)=\frac{(-1)^{n-1}(n-1)!}{(1+x)^n}.$$

Thus the required approximation is

$$f(0)+f'(0)x+\frac{f''(0)}{2!}x^2+\dots+\frac{f^{(n)}(0)}{n!}x^n$$
$$=x-\frac{x^2}{2}+\dots+(-1)^{n-1}\frac{x^n}{n}.$$

We emphasize that in these examples we are only concerned with approximations, valid for small values of x. Now we may look at Taylor's Theorem in a rather different way. By knowing the values of the derivatives of $f(x)$ at a point $x=a$, we are able to construct a polynomial approximating to it near a; in other words we are able to infer, with an accuracy depending on the number of values we know, the values of $f(x)$ at points near to a—we can trace the function back and we can predict it. It transpires that, for 'smooth' functions, we can achieve complete accuracy if we know all the derivatives. Then the approximating polynomial is replaced by a power series[1] whose sum equals the given function so long as the series continues to converge. Thus $\sin x$ is represented by the power series

$$x - \frac{x^3}{3!} + \ldots + (-1)^n \frac{x^{2n+1}}{(2n+1)!} + \ldots$$

everywhere; $\cos x$ is represented by the power series

$$1 - \frac{x^2}{2!} + \ldots + (-1)^n \frac{x^{2n}}{2n!} + \ldots$$

everywhere; and $\log(1+x)$ is represented by the power series

$$x - \frac{x^2}{2} + \ldots + (-1)^{n-1} \frac{x^n}{n} + \ldots$$

if $-1 < x \leqslant 1$.

We have used the word 'smooth' here in a deliberately vague sense; the point is that not all functions can be represented by power series, even those which possess all their derivatives may fail in this respect. The reader may rest assured that he is unlikely to meet such an unpleasant animal, but to show him that the difficulty is not one of the mathematician's invention, we will consider the function $e^{-\frac{1}{x^2}}$.

More precisely, let $f(x) = e^{-\frac{1}{x^2}}$, $x \neq 0$, $f(0) = 0$. Now it may be shown without difficulty that $\lim\limits_{x \to 0} \dfrac{e^{-\frac{1}{x^2}}}{x^m} = 0$, for any m. From this we may deduce that $f^{(n)}(0) = 0$ and that $f^{(n)}(x)$ is of the form $P_n\left(\dfrac{1}{x}\right) e^{-\frac{1}{x^2}}$ if $x \neq 0$, where P_n is a polynomial. The argument is by induction on n. We conclude that the polynomial of degree n approximating to $e^{-\frac{1}{x^2}}$ is 0!! Thus $e^{-\frac{1}{x^2}}$ is 'smaller' than any polynomial and indeed than any power series.

[1] See J. A. Green, *Sequences and Series*, in this series.

3. MAXIMA AND MINIMA

A most important application of Taylor's Theorem is to the question of maxima and minima. We recall from Theorem 3.3 that if $f(x)$ has a maximum or minimum at $x=c$, then $f'(c)=0$. We recall too that such a maximum (or minimum) is local in the sense that $f(c)>f(x)$, provided x belongs to some interval $a\leqslant x\leqslant b$, of which c is an interior point. Thus the criterion provided by the vanishing of the derivative is inapplicable to a maximum or minimum *located at an endpoint of an interval*. Thus, for example, if one is asked for the maximum of x^2 in $0\leqslant x\leqslant 1$, one may deduce from the criterion that there is no maximum in the interior of the interval, but there is obviously a maximum (in the ordinary sense of the word) at $x=1$, even though the derivative does not vanish there. Having given this warning, we will now confine ourselves to local maxima and minima in our strict sense.

Suppose now that $f'(a)=0$. Then by Taylor's Theorem,

$$f(x)=f(a)=\frac{(x-a)^2}{2}f''(\xi), \tag{3.5}$$

where ξ lies between x and a. Suppose further that $f''(a)\neq 0$, and that $f''(x)$ is continuous at $x=a$. Then $f''(x)$ has the same sign as $f''(a)$ if x is sufficiently near to a. Thus, for x sufficiently near to a, the sign of $f(x)-f(a)$ is the same as the sign of $\frac{(x-a)^2}{2}f''(a)$, that is, as the sign of $f''(a)$. We have thus proved

Theorem 3.11. *If $f(x)$ has a maximum or minimum at $x=a$, then $f'(a)=0$. If $f'(a)=0$, $f''(a)<0$, then $f(x)$ has a maximum at $x=a$; if $f'(a)=0$, $f''(a)>0$, then $f(x)$ has a minimum at $x=a$.*

We will say that $x=a$ is a *stationary* point if $f'(a)=0$; the reason for the terminology is clear, since the 'rate of change' of $f(x)$ at $x=a$ is zero.

Example 3.9. Show that $x(1-x)$ has a maximum at $x=\frac{1}{2}$.

For if $f(x)=x-x^2$, then $f'(x)=1-2x$, $f''(x)=-2$, so that $f'(\frac{1}{2})=0$, $f''(\frac{1}{2})<0$. Note that the maximum is $\frac{1}{4}$; this example says that the rectangle of given perimeter enclosing the maximum area is a square.

Example 3.10. A closed hollow cylinder on a circular base is to be made to contain a given volume V. Find the shape of the cylinder if the amount of material used is to be a minimum.

Let the radius of the base be r and let the height be h. Then $V = \pi r^2 h$. Since the cylinder is closed (at each end) the surface area S is given by

$$S = 2\pi rh + 2\pi r^2.$$

Thus the problem is to minimize $2\pi rh + 2\pi r^2$, subject to $V = \pi r^2 h$. We may simplify the algebra by saying that the problem is to minimize $rh + r^2$, subject to $r^2 h = c$. Let

$$f(r) = r^2 + r \cdot \frac{c}{r^2} = r^2 + \frac{c}{r}. \text{ Then } f'(r) = 2r - \frac{c}{r^2} = 0 \text{ if } 2r^3 = c.$$

Moreover, $f''(r) = 2 + \frac{2c}{r^3} > 0$ for all r. Thus a minimum is given

by $2r^3 = c$; but then $2r^3 = r^2 h$, so that $h = 2r$. Thus the surface area, and hence amount of material, is a minimum if the height is equal to the base diameter. Notice that this is the minimum in the ordinary sense of the word since $f(r)$ increases indefinitely as $r \to 0$ and as r increases indefinitely. Thus there is certainly no other minimum.

This last remark exemplifies an important general fact. Suppose we are looking for maxima or minima in the interval $a \leqslant x \leqslant b$ (we allow $a = -\infty$ or $b = \infty$ or both to indicate that the interval is unrestricted in the negative or positive direction or both). Then if our criterion gives us just one maximum this must be the 'overall' maximum for the whole interval unless it happens that there is an 'overall' maximum at a or b. This latter possibility occurs only if there is also a minimum. Precisely, suppose $f(x)$ has a maximum at $x = c$ and an 'overall' maximum at $x = b$. Then $f'(x)$ is negative immediately after c and positive just before b (this means 'positive for large x' if $b = \infty$), so that $f'(x)$, being continuous, vanishes between c and b and the first such point must be a minimum; thus we see that a minimum always appears between two maxima, as is geometrically obvious. A similar statement, in which 'maxima' and 'minima' are interchanged, also holds, of course.

Finally we take up the possibility, excluded in Theorem 3.11, that $f''(a)$ vanishes at a stationary point a. In fact, let us suppose that $f'(a)=f''(a)=\ldots=f^{(n-1)}(a)=0$, $n\geqslant 2$, but $f^{(n)}(a)\neq 0$. Then (compare (3.5))

$$f(x)-f(a)=\frac{(x-a)^n}{n!}f^{(n)}(\xi) \tag{3.6}$$

where ξ lies between x and a. As before, we conclude that, if x is sufficiently near to a, then the sign of $f(x)-f(a)$ is the same as that of $\frac{(x-a)^n}{n!}f^{(n)}(a)$.

Now it is clear that the crucial question is whether n is odd or even. If n is even, the sign of $f(x)-f(a)$ is the same as that of $f^{(n)}(a)$, so that $f(a)$ is a minimum if $f^{(n)}(a)>0$, and a maximum if $f^{(n)}(a)<0$. On the other hand, if n is odd, $f(x)-f(a)$ changes sign as x passes from the left of $a(x<a)$ to the right of $a(x>a)$, so that $f(a)$ is neither a maximum or a minimum.

Theorem 3.12. *Let $x=a$ be a stationary point of $f(x)$. Then $f(a)$ is a maximum (minimum) if the first derivative which does not vanish at $x=a$ is $f^{(n)}(a)$, where n is even and $f^{(n)}(a)$ is negative (positive). If the first non-vanishing derivative is $f^{(n)}(a)$, where n is odd, then $f(a)$ is neither a maximum nor a minimum.*

The obvious example is provided by $f(x)=x^m$, $m\geqslant 2$. Then $x=0$ is a stationary point. The first non-vanishing derivative $f^{(n)}(0)$ is given by $n=m$, when $f^{(m)}(0)=m!$ Thus x^m has a minimum at the origin if and only if m is given. This is quite obvious geometrically from the shape of the graph of $y=x^m$.

Actually, Theorem 3.12 is not quite exhaustive; it is exhaustive for 'smooth' functions in the sense of the previous section, but we immediately see that our old friend

$$f(x)=e^{-\frac{1}{x^2}},\ x\neq 0,\ f(0)=0$$

escapes the net. For obviously $f(x)$ has a minimum at the origin, since e^x is always positive, but there are no non-vanishing derivatives at the origin.

We close with a practical hint. It is often very tedious to compute the second derivative $f''(x)$ at a stationary point.

47

However, if we can show that $f'(x)$ is increasing as x passes through a (from negative values through zero to positive values) we may conclude that $f(a)$ is minimum, and similarly for a maximum.

Example 3.11. Find the maxima and minima of $\dfrac{1-x}{3+x^2}$.

Let

$$f(x) = \frac{1-x}{3+x^2}; \text{ then } f'(x) = \frac{(3+x^2)(-1)-(1-x)(2x)}{(3+x^2)^2} = \frac{x^2-2x-3}{(3+x^2)^2}.$$

Thus $f'(x) = 0$ if $x^2 - 2x - 3 = 0$, that is, if $x = -1$ or 3. Now it is a general theorem that the quadratic expression (or polynomial) $ax^2 + bx + c$ has the same sign as a except when x lies between the roots of $ax^2 + bx + c$. Thus $f'(x) > 0$ if $x < -1$, $f'(x) < 0$ if $x > -1$ (but near to -1), and $f'(x) < 0$ if $x < 3$ (but near to 3), $f'(x) > 0$ if $x > 3$. It follows that $f(x)$ has a maximum value of $\frac{1}{2}$ at $x = -1$, and a minimum value of $-\frac{1}{6}$ at $x = 3$.

4. NEWTON'S METHOD FOR THE APPROXIMATE SOLUTION OF EQUATIONS

In this final section we give a further important application of Taylor's Theorem. We have

$$f(a+h) = f(a) + hf'(a) + \frac{h^2}{2}f''(a+\theta h). \tag{3.7}$$

Now suppose $f(a+h) = 0$; then, if $f'(a) \neq 0$,

$$h = -\frac{f(a)}{f'(a)} - \frac{h^2}{2}\frac{f''(a+\theta h)}{f'(a)}.$$

If we further suppose that h is small, so that $\dfrac{h^2}{2}\dfrac{f''(a+\theta h)}{f'(a)}$ is small compared with $\dfrac{f(a)}{f'(a)}$, we conclude that $-\dfrac{f(a)}{f'(a)}$ is a good approximation to h. In practice, then, we assume that $x = a$ is an approximate solution of $f(x) = 0$ and we then expect $x = a - \dfrac{f(a)}{f'(a)}$ to be a better approximation. Notice that if

$h_0 = -\dfrac{f(a)}{f'(a)}$, then (3.7) gives

$$f(a_1) = \frac{(f(a))^2}{2(f'(a))^2} \cdot f''(a+\theta h_0),$$

where $a_1 = a + h_0$. Thus $\dfrac{f(a_1)}{f(a)} = \dfrac{f(a) \cdot f''(a+\theta h_0)}{2(f'(a))^2}$, and provided that

$x = a$ was a reasonable approximation to a root of $f(x) = 0$, the right-hand side will be small, so that $f(a_1)$ will be small compared with $f(a)$. Obviously the method works best when f' is large.

Geometrically, the procedure is as follows. Let P be the point $(a, f(a))$ on $y = f(x)$. The tangent at P is $y - f(a) = f'(a)(x-a)$ and this meets the x-axis at $\left(a - \dfrac{f(a)}{f'(a)}, 0\right) = (a_1, 0)$. To repeat the procedure we take P_1 to be $(a_1, f(a_1))$ and find where the tangent at P_1 meets the x-axis (see Fig. 7).

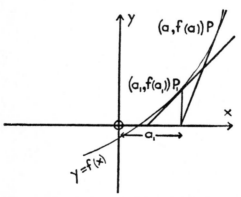

Fig. 7.—Newton's method for solving $f(x) = 0$.

It is to be emphasized that this method should only be used if it is known that there is a root of $f(x) = 0$ in the neighbourhood of $x = a$. In other words, the starting point for the application of Newton's method must be chosen with foresight.

Example 3.12. Find a solution of $x^3 - 3x - 11 = 0$, correct to 2 places of decimals.

Put $f(x) = x^3 - 3x - 11$. Then $f(2) = -9$, $f(3) = 7$. Thus there a root between $x = 2$ and $x = 3$. We have $f(x) = x^3 - 3x - 11$, $f'(x) = 3x^2 - 3$. Try $a = 3$. Then

$$h_0 = -\frac{f(a)}{f'(a)} = -\frac{7}{24} = -\cdot3 \text{ (approx.).}$$

Thus we take $a_1 = 2\cdot7$; then

$$h_1 = -\frac{\cdot583}{18\cdot87} = -\cdot031 \text{ (approx.).}$$

Take $a_2 = 2\cdot669$; then $h_2 = -\dfrac{\cdot01}{18\cdot375} = -\cdot0005$ (approx.).

It is thus reasonable to suppose that $x = 2\cdot67$ is a solution to 2 places of decimals. This is proved by the further observation that $f(2\cdot665) < 0$, since we know that $f(2\cdot675) > 0$.

EXERCISES ON CHAPTER III

Find the maxima and minima of

1. $3x^2 - 12x + 5$. 2. $(3 + x)(1 - x)$. 3. $2x^4 - 2x^3 - 7x^2 + 3$.

4. $x^4 - 4x^3 + 10$. 5. $\frac{1}{5}x^5 - \frac{1}{4}x^4$. 6. $\log x - 2x^2$.

7. $e^x(1 - x)$. 8. $\dfrac{1}{1 + x} + x$. 9. $\sinh x - \sin x$.

10. $4 \cos x + 3 \sin x$. 11. $\cot x + 4 \tan x$. 12. $\dfrac{\cos x}{1 + \cot x}$.

13. $\tan x - 8 \sin x$. 14. $\sin 2x + 7 \sin x$. 15. $e^x \sin x$.

16. The curves $y = x^4 + 2x^3 - 18x^2 + 63$, $y = 9x^2 - 45$ touch. Find their point of contact and their other points of intersection.

17. Prove that if a is a zero of the polynomial $f(x)$ and an $(m-1)$-fold zero of $f'(x)$, then it is an m-fold zero of $f(x)$.

18. Find $\lim\limits_{x \to 0} \dfrac{\log(1 + x + x^2) - x}{\sin^2 x}$. 19. Find $\lim\limits_{x \to 0} \dfrac{e^{\sin 2x} - 1}{x}$.

20. Find $\lim\limits_{x \to 0} \dfrac{\tan x - \sin x}{\tan x - x}$.

21. Approximate to tan $2x$ by a polynomial in x of degree 5.

22. Approximate to sec x by a polynomial in x of degree 4.

23. Approximate to x cosec x by a polynomial in x of degree 4.

24. Approximate to $(\log (1+x))^2$ by a polynomial in x of degree 4.

Hence or otherwise evaluate $\lim\limits_{x \to 0} \dfrac{(\log (1+x))^2 - x^2}{x(1 - \cos x)}$.

25. Prove that $f(x) = \tanh^{-1} x$ satisfies $(1 - x^2)f'(x) - 1 = 0$. Deduce that
$$(1 - x^2)f^{(n)}(x) - 2(n-1)xf^{(n-1)}(x) - (n-1)(n-2)f^{(n-2)}(x) = 0,$$
and hence approximate to $\tanh^{-1} x$ by a polynomial in x of degree $(2k+1)$.

26. The function $f(x)$ satisfies $f'''(x) - f''(x) + 2f'(x) - f(x) = 0$ and $f(0) = 0$, $f'(0) = 1$, $f''(0) = 0$. Approximate to $f(x)$ by a polynomial in x of degree 6.

27. By Taylor's Theorem,
$$f(x) = f(0) + xf'(0) + \ldots + \frac{x^{n-1}}{(n-1)!}f^{(n-1)}(0) + \frac{x^n}{n!}f^{(n)}(\theta x), 0 < \theta < 1.$$
Show that if $f^{(n+1)}(x)$ is continuous and $f^{(n+1)}(0)$ o, then θ is a single-valued function of x for x sufficiently small.

28. Find a solution, correct to 2 places of decimals, of
$$x^3 - 8x + 6 = 0,$$
near to $x = 2$.

29. Find a solution, correct to 2 places of decimals, of
$$x^4 - x - 1 = 0,$$
near to $x = 1$.

30. Find a solution, correct to 2 places of decimals, of
$$x^2 - 10 \log_e x = 0,$$
near to $x = 3$.

ANSWERS TO EXERCISES

CHAPTER II

1. $3x^2 + 6x$. 2. $30x^5 - 30x^4$. 3. $2x^3 + 27x^2$.

4. $\dfrac{1 - 2x - x^2}{(x^2 + 1)^2}$. 5. $\dfrac{\frac{1}{2}x^{-\frac{1}{4}} + \frac{1}{2}x^{-\frac{1}{2}} + 6x + 15x^{\frac{2}{3}}}{(3x^{\frac{2}{3}} + 1)^2}$.

6. $2 \sin x \cos x$. 7. $-3 \sin 3x$.

8. $\dfrac{1}{1 + 2x + 2x^2} - 2x \cos x^2$. 9. $\sin^{-1} x + \dfrac{x}{\sqrt{(1 - x^2)}}$.

10. $\dfrac{2(1 - 4x^2)^{-\frac{1}{2}}}{x - 1} + \dfrac{\cos^{-1} 2x}{(x - 1)^2}$. 11. ae^{ax+b}. 12. $e^x e^{e^x}$.

13. e. 14. $\cot x$. 15. $\dfrac{1}{x \log x}$.

16. $x^{x^x}(x^{x-1} + x^x \log x(1 + \log x))$. 17. $5 \sinh 5x$.

18. $\tanh x$. 19. $\dfrac{1}{2} - \dfrac{1}{2x^2}$.

20. $f'(x) = 2x \sin \dfrac{1}{x} - \cos \dfrac{1}{x}$, $x \neq 0$, $f'(0) = 0$.

21. $t^2 y + x = 2ct$. 22. $(y - y(t_0))x'(t_0) = (x - x(t_0))y'(t_0)$.

24. $\dfrac{g(gf'' - fg'') - 2g'(gf' - fg')}{g^3}$.

25. If $p(x) = f_1(x) f_2(x) \ldots f_n(x)$, then $p'(x) = f_1'(x) f_2(x) \ldots f_n(x) + f_1(x) f_2'(x) \ldots f_n(x) + \ldots + f_1(x) f_2(x) \ldots f_n'(x)$.

26. False for rational functions.

27. $x = \pi - \sin^{-1} y$, $\dfrac{dx}{dy} = -\dfrac{1}{\sqrt{(1 - y^2)}}$.

28. $x = -\cos^{-1} y$, $\dfrac{dx}{dy} = \dfrac{1}{\sqrt{(1 - y^2)}}$.

29. $\sin x \sec^2 x$, $-\cos x \operatorname{cosec}^2 x$, $-\operatorname{cosec}^2 x$, $-\sinh x \operatorname{sech}^2 x$, $-\cosh x \operatorname{cosech}^2 x$, $-\operatorname{cosech}^2 x$.

30. $\log\left(\dfrac{1}{x}+\sqrt{\dfrac{1}{x^2}-1}\right)$, $\log\left(\dfrac{1}{x}+\sqrt{\dfrac{1}{x^2}+1}\right)$, $\tfrac{1}{2}\log\dfrac{x+1}{x-1}$;

$$\dfrac{-1}{x\sqrt{1-x^2}}, \quad \dfrac{-1}{x\sqrt{1+x^2}}, \quad \dfrac{1}{1-x^2}.$$

CHAPTER III

1. Min. at $x=2$, value -7. 2. Max. at $x=-1$, value 4.

3. Max. at $x=0$, value 3; min. at $x=-1$, value 0;

   min. at $x=\dfrac{7}{4}$, value $-\dfrac{1331}{128}$.

4. Min. at $x=3$, value -17.

5. Min. at $x=1$, value $-\dfrac{1}{20}$; max. at $x=0$, value 0.

6. Max. at $x=\tfrac{1}{2}$, value $-\log 2 - \tfrac{1}{2}$.

7. Max. at $x=0$, value 1.

8. Max. at $x=-2$, value -3; min. at $x=0$, value 1.

9. No max. or min.

10. Max. at $x=\alpha$, where $\cos\alpha=\tfrac{4}{5}$, $\sin\alpha=\tfrac{3}{5}$, value 5;
    min. at $x=\pi+\alpha$, value -5.

11. Min. at $\tan x=\tfrac{1}{2}$, value 4; max. at $\tan x=-\tfrac{1}{2}$, value -4.

12. Max. at $x=\dfrac{\pi}{4}$, value $\dfrac{1}{2\sqrt{2}}$; min. at $x=\dfrac{5\pi}{4}$, value $-\dfrac{1}{2\sqrt{2}}$.

13. Min. at $x=\dfrac{\pi}{3}$, value $-3\sqrt{3}$; max. at $x=-\dfrac{\pi}{3}$, value $3\sqrt{3}$.

14. Max. at $x=\alpha$, where $\cos\alpha=\dfrac{1}{4}$, $\sin\alpha=\dfrac{\sqrt{15}}{4}$, value $\left(\dfrac{\sqrt{15}}{2}\right)^3$;

    min. at $x=-\alpha$, value $-\left(\dfrac{\sqrt{15}}{2}\right)^3$.

15. Max. at $x=n\pi+\dfrac{3\pi}{4}$, n even, min. at $x=n\pi+\dfrac{3\pi}{4}$, n odd;
    value $\dfrac{(-1)^n}{\sqrt{2}}e^{n\pi+\frac{3\pi}{4}}$.

16. $(3,36)$; $(-2, -9)$, $(-6, 279)$.   18. $\frac{1}{2}$.   19. 2.   20. $\frac{3}{2}$.

21. $2x + \dfrac{8x^3}{3} + \dfrac{64x^5}{15}$.   22. $1 + \dfrac{x^2}{2} + \dfrac{5x^4}{24}$.   23. $1 + \dfrac{x^2}{6} + \dfrac{7x^4}{360}$.

24. $x^2 - x^3 + \dfrac{11x^4}{12}$; -2.   25. $x + \dfrac{x^3}{3} + \dots + \dfrac{x^{2k+1}}{2k+1}$.

26. $x - \dfrac{x^3}{3} - \dfrac{x^4}{24} + \dfrac{x^5}{40} + \dfrac{x^6}{240}$.   28. 2·33.   29. 1·22.   30. 3·57.

Index